ROLY'S BISTRO

THE RESTAURANT AND ITS FOOD

ROLY'S BISTRO

THE RESTAURANT AND ITS FOOD

Colin O'Daly
Paul Cartwright

PHOTOGRAPHS: NEIL MACDOUGALD

GILL & MACMILLAN

Gill & Macmillan Ltd
Hume Avenue, Park West
Dublin 12
with associated companies throughout the world
www.gillmacmillan.ie
© Colin O'Daly 2002
0 7171 3434 2
Index compiled by Cover To Cover
Design and print origination by
Slick Fish Design, Dublin
Colour reproduction by Ultragraphics Ltd, Dublin
Printed by GraphyCems Ltd, Spain

This book is typeset in Helvetica and Frutiger.

The paper used in this book comes from the wood pulp of managed forests. For every tree felled, at least one tree is planted, thereby renewing natural resources.

A CIP catalogue record for this book is available from the
British Library.

1 3 5 4 2

Acknowledgments

With thanks to John Mulcahy whose idea the Bistro was in the first place.

Special thanks to the valued staff of Roly's who make it happen seven days a week.

Thanks also to Eveleen Coyle and Deirdre McQuillan for their unfailing help and patience in bringing this book together.

Contents

Spring 28

Summer   52

Autumn

Winter 98

Note: All the recipes in this book have been tested in domestic kitchens by home cooks.

Introduction

Roly's Bistro opened its doors to the public in a brand new redbrick building in Dublin's Ballsbridge on Wednesday, 11 November 1992. Ten big sash windows with blinds proclaiming the name, and a daffodil-yellow dining room with crisp white tablecloths, offered a welcoming feeling of cheerfulness, freshness and light. What had started as an idea floated by John Mulcahy (a well-known figure in the catering industry) to John O'Sullivan and Roly Saul one late night in a Cascais restaurant during a golfing holiday, suddenly became a reality. It was a confident undertaking at a time when Ireland was in recession and some of the city's best-known restaurants were closing down; my own in Blackrock had shut its doors a year previously. All of our team brought different professional skills and experience to the venture. Our culinary goal was a simple but challenging one: to bring high standards to a wider audience, to present *haute cuisine* at ready-to-wear prices, so to speak. The idea was to offer a reasonably priced seasonal menu with freshly cooked food and inexpensive mainstream wines in a casual bistro-style atmosphere, without compromising on quality, seven days a week. Staff stood by with their orders and long white aprons.

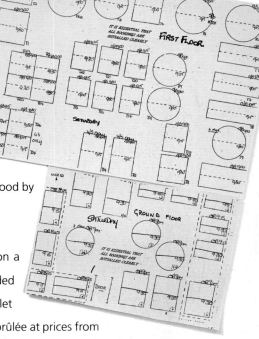

The menu was our mission statement. Printed on a large stiff card, bistro style, its suggestions included among others, prawn bisque, roast rack of lamb, fillet of pork with prune and armagnac sauce and crème brûlée at prices from around £2 for starters, £8 for main courses and £2.50 for desserts.

Everything was, and is, cooked to order. The wine list contained ten house wines for £9.50 and a careful selection of familiar French, Italian, Spanish and world wines, the most expensive of which was £25.

Roly's got an enthusiastic send-off and many well-known personalities including Mary Robinson, then President of Ireland, came in to wish it success. I remember being close to God that day, getting used to a new kitchen, new staff and a new system. You don't know your team or its strength until it is put to the test, until it is thrust into the front line under pressure. We served 120 satisfied customers on those first two nights and sighed with relief. Our telephone number started to ring encouragingly.

Ten years on, it rings incessantly and we can claim with some degree of pride that our formula has worked. Roly Saul has since gone on to open his own place while we remain a popular and much-loved Dublin restaurant frequented by international celebrities, local residents, romantic couples, family groups, old age pensioners and business associates. Well-known regulars include Bono and Ali Hewson, Enya, The Corrs, Keith Wood, Seamus and Marie Heaney, and, when they're in Dublin, Liam Neeson, Sting, Kylie Minogue, Stephen Hendry, Ken Doherty and Michael Caine, to name but a few. We were the sole Dublin nomination for the TV3 Viewers' Choice Award at the Bushmills Malt Irish Restaurant Awards 2002.

Open 361 days a year, it's a busy restaurant that serves over three thousand people a week. Our menu is geared to conservative as well as changing tastes, to comfort food as well as reworked classics, always based on top quality ingredients. An industrious army of 27 chefs backstage works from early morning to late at night to prepare and serve food of a standard that is consistent and reliable and at prices we believe are incomparable. Our customers are our priority and more than a third of them are regulars; one couple came in every day for lunch, and dinner twice a week, for years.

Paul Cartwright joined us as head chef in 1996 and brought a new youthfulness and sense of organisation to the place. He became general manager in January 2000. A Dubliner, he trained in Ireland and France and worked with Anton Edelman at the Savoy in London for nearly five years in charge of 100 chefs every night where he learnt about the importance of care and attention to detail. We work well together as a team and he has enabled me to take more of a front-of-house role. John O'Sullivan, our managing director, and his wife Angela, a microbiologist, are equally involved in the day-to-day running of the restaurant.

A restaurant kitchen is not like a domestic kitchen and ours is phenomenally demanding and driven. It is a stainless steel pressure chamber in which every chef works on his or her station — often referred to as the Stations of the Cross — preparing soups, sauces, garnishes, stocks, chopping vegetables, cutting up meat and the flesh of fish and fowl.

The Working Day

The working day begins early. The first person to open up at 6 a.m. just before the milkman arrives is usually Matt Byrne, now in his seventies. Trained in Paris and in the Café Royal in London, he was sous chef in Dublin's legendary Russell Hotel and head chef in the Metropole for ten years. Our sous chef on duty will join him along with seven other chefs, and by 10 a.m. the place is humming.

At the soup and sauce station, prawn bisque is prepared in enormous 75 litre metal cauldrons, while leek and potato soup and other stocks are already simmering and vegetables roasting in a pan. We make around 40–50 litres of stock daily. Steel guns are used to prepare pesto in huge buckets. Other chefs work on salads and starters. Supplies arrive from around 8.30 a.m. and everything is checked. Our staff come from Ireland and all over the world — from Spain, Italy, China, France, South Africa, Zimbabwe and Romania — a real ethnic melting pot, each contributing in their own way to the smooth running of the operation.

Three or four boxes of fresh prawns are bought daily, all of them peeled at the central table and kept chilled, ready for the pan. Nothing is cooked in advance except our lamb pie; it is a traditional Kerry lamb pie but with white wine (which certainly would not have been traditional in Kerry). It has been one of our most popular dishes since we opened and takes 20 minutes to finish in the oven before serving.

Our menu generally offers a choice of eight starters and 11 main courses, with two or three specials. We believe in supplying what the general public *want* and respond to changing eating habits. In 2000, for example, 30 per cent of people wanted fish and 70 per cent opted for meat dishes. Now the ratio is 40–45 per cent fish to 55–60 per cent meat. Fish is more expensive than fillet of beef now; we spend around €8,000 a week on fish alone. Paul Cartwright always starts preparing it first, wielding his knives and fish tweezers with the sort of speed and expertise that comes from years of practice.

As Chef de Cuisine, the first thing Paul does in the morning is check the figures from the day before, how many covers we did and whether there were any problems or difficulties. We use the Hygiene Analysis Critical Control Points (HACCP) system of hygiene control which means keeping a strict note of fridge, fish and air temperatures, for example. We also keep a record of everything we cook which is regularly analysed by our food scientist, Dr Ted Hood; all our chopping boards are colour coded — blue for fish, red for meat and green for vegetables. Around

€25,000 a week is spent on raw materials; we buy by the day, and sell by the day, and every Monday at 7.30 a.m. Gerry Butler carries out a detailed stock take. He combines ordering from our suppliers with cheffing and enjoys the variety.

By 12 o'clock all our supplies are in for the day; the prawns are shelled, tomatoes for garnish chopped, over a hundred chicken breasts tidied up, filo pastry wrapped around confit of duck, mayonnaise finished and sauces ready. We use about a dozen 12 lb bags of potatoes a day and serve about 400 fillet steaks a week, sometimes more — mostly to men and many still want them well done. Each piece of monkfish or salmon is weighed and wrapped in cling film — we never serve tails of any fish and use all the trimmings for fish cakes or terrines. I don't think you would find monkfish at our price on any other restaurant menu in Dublin. Everything we cook, we taste — all the sauces and all the dressings. Before a new item goes on the menu it is cooked, tasted and costed.

First customers start arriving around 12.10 where they will be greeted by John or Angela or by our front-of-house managers Áine Levins or Liam Guerin. John and Angela were the first in Ireland to introduce a restaurant software package when they owned Blake's in 1983; they also mapped our seating charts. All the cutlery on the restaurant tables will have been polished twice, and glasses and table settings checked and double-checked.

People love sitting at the window tables because of the great views. Table 2 overlooks the garden and you could be on the Champs Élysées; it's a great place for people-watching. Table 6 is a circular one that seats six to eight and you feel like you are at the captain's table because you can see the whole room. Sometimes there's more action under the table than over it! Table 15 is a good one when you're not on anyone's menu except your own, and table 22 is one I personally like when I am alone because you have your back to the wall, you can read the paper and see everything that's going on. Table 106 is perfect for two and is right in the middle of the restaurant — it's quite a romantic table. Tables 12 and

14 are private booths. We operate a staggered seating arrangement to suit the kitchen, which means that tables can be filled twice in the evening. It works out very well when you are dealing with so many customers.

Orders from the waiting staff are given to the expeditor who immediately calls them out to the chefs. At 12.30 the first starters are dispatched with a cry from the kitchen of 'starters away'. It's usually a gentle beginning as we remove roast pork from the oven and put in lamb pies, start cooking the meat or fish orders, fill the vegetable dishes or blowtorch the crèmes brûlées. It gets hectic but in a *mis en place* kitchen if you don't tidy as you go, there would be complete chaos. The lunch menu, being relatively simple, enables us to serve 100 people in an hour.

When an order is called in to the kitchen, the drill is to stop whatever you are doing and put the request in the oven or on the pan. 'Four steak fillets' — on the pan. 'Three hake' — on the pan. A chef in full spate must do many things at once: remove a fillet of fish from the fridge drawer, shake salt on chips, remember the timing on an oven dish, pour gravy on a plate and assemble the finished dish (called 'plating up') before it is sent out. There will be ten people doing ten different jobs in fast-moving co-ordination and a huge, noisy clatter of plates and cutlery. The kitchen porter will be elbow deep in hot water, washing each pan as it is used; a pastry chef will be putting the final swirls and snowy icing sugar to a dessert order. Outside in the restaurant, fast-moving waiters and runners are attending to the clientele and there's a noisy hum of conversation.

The restaurant business is like showtime and at night our curtain raisers come in around 6 o'clock. The most popular time for eating out in Dublin is between 8 and 9 o'clock when the pace in the kitchen builds up to a crescendo, becoming intensely hot and concentrated for about an hour and a half. There are two completely contrasting atmospheres in the building at this time. There's the noisy chatter in the bar and the animated conversation and laughter in the restaurant, while backstage it's a whirl of activity as orders are dispatched and trays with empty plates and glasses are returned by the waiting staff. Plates go in, plates go out, and fridge doors are opened and closed amid a frenetic sense of urgency, speed and concentration. By 10.20 any night a full restaurant of people will have been served by a team of 70 staff. A little girl celebrating her birthday will be presented with a specially made birthday cake and will curl in delight as the staff sing 'Happy Birthday'. The details count as much as the bigger picture.

As the evening draws to a close, the pace will slacken, waiters will clear tables and chefs will reach for a cup of tea before going home. Last to depart are the manager and the barman and outside everything seems to slow down and cars appear to roll past. You look down the road from the restaurant towards the US Embassy and it's like an empty runway with bright lights lined up on either side. A lone sentry walks back and forth like a pendulum and as the clock on the church strikes the hour Ballsbridge returns to being a village for a short while.

Such is the end of a working day, but as Roly's celebrates its tenth birthday this year, we mark our move into the next decade with a brand new extension which includes a private dining room seating up to a hundred people and an outdoor catering service. Busy times, as always, lie ahead.

Roly's by Numbers

Bottles of **wine** sold annually 56,784

Bottles of **champagne** sold annually 988

Price of **prawns** on the menu **1992** €15.87
Price of **prawns** on the menu **2002** €24.06

Price of **lamb pie 1992** €11.36
Price of **lamb pie 2002** €17.71

Potatoes bought annually 35,380 kg

Prawns bought annually 4,420 kg

Flour bought annually 26,000 kg

Roly's Wine List — Vintage Tales

Our wine list is as carefully chosen as our menu. When we opened, its quality and value for money was a talking point and we try to keep it that way, responding to changing tastes where necessary. Prices are affordable, labels familiar and our choice, selected from around the world, caters for every customer: a young couple out on a date, a husband and wife celebrating an anniversary, or a business person impressing a client. Our policy of a low mark up on wines and of taking a smaller percentage on higher value wines is consistent with our food pricing, and we were one of the first restaurants in Ireland to offer a house selection.

The current list offers excellent value house wine, Jean Louis Chancel from the southern Rhône. For the more discerning wine drinker there are two additional house selections from Europe and the New World: fourteen reds and fourteen whites. The main list has a selection of some 40 bottles priced from around €22 for a Penfolds Chardonnay up to a Chateau Lynch Bages 1996 at under €100. In keeping with current tastes and trends, most wines are young, recent vintages and from the New World. Ten years ago when we opened, France represented 54 per cent of the market; today that percentage is 32, and that change is reflected in our list.

There are still many wines from France: well-known white wines like Chablis Grand Cru Les Clos Regnard 1997, Corton Charlemagne Louis Latour 1998, and, from the Loire, the very special Pouilly Fumée 1997 of Baron de Ladoucette. From New Zealand, there's the award-winning Sauvignon Blanc from Hunters, the company founded by Ernie Hunter from Northern Ireland which is now run by his wife Jane. This wine was served at a dinner in Dublin Castle in honour of the New Zealand Prime Minister, James Bolger, in 1993.

The red wine list is well balanced, offering a Drouhin Fleurie from Beaujolais and Chateau Loudenne from Bordeaux, to Chateau Lynch Bages 1996 and the Vosne Romanée Louis Latour 1996, exceptional value at the top end. New World wines include the South African Klein Constantia, Wolf Blass from Australia, and Navarra Correas from Argentina. Lovers of champagne can choose from Taittinger Brut Réserve or Louis Roederer Cristal at prices we reckon can't be bettered.

We make a point of visiting vineyards to select our wines, and in the past few years have started special gourmet wine dinners; their success indicates the growing level of interest in wine in Ireland. Each event is introduced by a different winemaker from France, South Africa or Australia. We create a special seven-course menu for the occasion to accompany seven different wines, and we limit the evening to 50 people. More are planned for the future.

Roly's Bakery

Brown Bread

Cheese, Mustard Seed and Pumpkin Seed Bread

Mediterranean Bread

Roly's Birthday Cake

Warm Strawberry and Plum Crêpes

Gluten-Free Breads

    Basic White Dough

    Tomato and Fennel Bread

    Bacon and Onion Bread

    Pesto/Herb Bread

Built in 1996, our Bakery is where bread is freshly made every day as well as pastries and desserts for the restaurant. In an age of mass production, wholesome, hand-crafted bread is a quality product and our customers love it. 'Everybody in Ireland eats bread. It is one of the most important of all foods and people are much more conscious of quality now', says David Walsh who, with two assistants, heads a team of seven pastry chefs. Ten different varieties of loaves are made daily including plain white and brown as well as spinach and raisin, herb, mixed seed, red pepper and black olive, though customer favourites are apricot and walnut and tomato and fennel. Gluten-free bread is also baked.

The Bakery not only supplies the restaurant's dinner and lunch menus, but also Aer Lingus Premier Class, and 100 loaves go on public sale at the front door each morning at 10.30, a figure which more than doubles at weekends. Well-known fans of our crusty treats include John Hurt, Van Morrison, Robbie Coltrane and, while he was filming in *The General*, the US actor John Voight who is remembered for coming away from the Bakery laden with four bags of bread every day.

Variety and freshness are the goals of David Walsh, whose pride is that the last basket at night is the same as the first and that the restaurant has never run out of bread. Kitchen staff look forward to their morning elevenses — delicious hunks of freshly made rasher sandwiches which are devoured eagerly. All bread is rolled and finished by hand using special French bakers' knives to give distinctive designs, slashes or 'hedgehog' finishes to the crusts, and each loaf is individually cut and arranged in big wicker baskets before dispatch to the restaurant. The Bakery uses around 120 kilos of flour a day sourced from all over the country. All the ingredients are organic and no preservatives are used. Nothing is wasted.

Like the bread he makes, David Walsh is an early riser, driving into Ballsbridge from his home in Lucan every morning at 5.30. All the raw ingredients will have been measured, weighed and assembled the night before. The work is very precise and methodical and that precision means consistency. 'Bread is very scientific and once you understand the science you can get it right, but you must have respect for yeast', he says. Different seasons have different effects and in winter, for example, when it is really cold, the temperature of the water has to be warmer.

Seasonality also plays a part in deciding on dessert menus. Crèmes brûlées, pavlovas and chocolate dishes are customer favourites, and traditional desserts like tarts and compotes rather than more elaborate confections are becoming popular again. All sweet garnishes like sauces and custards are made in the morning and cheese is cut, wrapped in wet cotton and covered with cling film. In December there is a huge demand for sweet breads and brioches, mince pies and Christmas puddings. Birthday cakes are a year-round speciality made to order for restaurant celebrations.

David Walsh trained as a chef in Tallaght RTC, completed an advanced pastry course and took a National Culinary Arts Degree in l999. He also teaches. Having worked in restaurants in Cork and Galway, he started with us as a chef de parti (head of a section) in the kitchen and worked his way up, taking over the Bakery in 1998. As one who spends 12–13 hours a day at his work, what he loves most is creating his own recipes and the satisfaction of seeing all the raw ingredients in the morning converted to the finished products on the racks. We have included recipes for some of his most popular breads as well as gluten-free loaves and dessert crêpes.

Brown Bread

Our brown bread contains five different blends of flour and is our best seller.
Makes 2 loaves

850 ml buttermilk
375 g strong baker's flour
250 g coarse wholemeal
80 g pinhead oats
80 g oatflakes
80 g wheatgerm
20 g brown sugar
10 g salt
30 g bread soda
10 g melted butter
1 egg
1 teaspoon caraway seeds
2 teaspoons treacle

Preheat oven to 200°C/400°F/Gas 6. Use buttermilk that has been out of the fridge for one hour. Using a deep bowl, sieve the bread soda and white flour together, then mix in wholemeal flour, pinhead oats, oatflakes and wheatgerm with your hand. Add melted butter and treacle to the buttermilk. Make a centre in the middle of the flour and pour in buttermilk. With one hand mix vigorously until everything is incorporated with the buttermilk. The mix should be quite wet. Add the egg. Leave dough for about 5 minutes before baking to allow ingredients to settle and the bread soda to start working. Divide into 2 well-greased loaf tins and bake in the middle of the oven for 60–90 minutes until the bread has risen and dried out. Turn out on to a wire rack and allow to cool before cutting.

Cheese, Mustard Seed and Pumpkin Seed Bread

Makes 1 loaf

750 g strong flour
25 g unsalted butter
15 g sugar
30 g fresh yeast or 10 g dried yeast
1 teaspoon salt
430 ml warm water
30 g Stilton cheese
30 g pumpkin seeds
2 teaspoons wholegrain mustard
sesame seeds and egg wash
1 egg yolk
20 ml milk

Using a mixer with a dough hook, sieve the flour into the bowl on the lowest speed, adding the cheese, butter, sugar and salt. In another bowl, mix the yeast with the water, milk and egg yolk, making sure the yeast is fully broken down. The liquid should turn a pale grey. Gradually add the liquid into the flour, increasing the speed of the mixer until it forms a dough. This should take about 7 minutes, but if you do it by hand, you will have to knead for about 14 minutes. Turn off machine. If you use fresh yeast, cover the bowl with a clean damp cloth and leave to prove for about 40 minutes to one hour.* Preheat oven to 220°C/425°F/Gas 7. Remove cloth, put bowl back on to machine and mix the dough again to knock out all the air. Mix in mustard and pumpkin seeds until a dough ball is formed again. Remove dough and cut in half. Shape into round loaves or put into 2 lightly oiled tins and place on baking trays. Brush with egg wash and sprinkle with sesame seeds. Cut straight across using a blade and leave in a warm place covered with a tea towel for about 20–30 minutes. Bake for 30 minutes, adding a bowl of water to the bottom of the oven.

*Dried yeast does not require this proving. If using dried yeast, all the ingredients are added in the first mixing including the mustard and pumpkin seeds. When mixing is finished, shape straightaway and leave to prove until doubled in size.

Mediterranean Bread

Makes 1 loaf

750 g strong white flour
25 g unsalted butter
25 g sugar
35 g fresh yeast
1 teaspoon salt
20 g sun-dried tomatoes
75 g black pitted olives
75 g mixed peppers, diced
4 anchovy fillets
100 g tomato purée
300 ml warm water
20 ml milk
1 egg

In a small bowl, mix the yeast with 100 ml water and sugar and 100 g of the flour and leave for 5–7 minutes. Sieve the rest of the flour into a mixing bowl and add salt, sun-dried tomatoes and butter. Add tomato purée to the rest of the water, then egg and milk. Gradually add all the liquids to the dry ingredients in a mixer until a dough is formed, which should take about 10–12 minutes. Turn off machine, cover with a damp cloth and allow to prove for about 80 minutes in warm conditions — the dough

should double in size. Remove cloth, return bowl to mixer, add the peppers, anchovies and olives, increasing the speed until the dough is mixed and leaving the sides of the bowl. The peppers should be quite small and fully incorporated. Turn off machine and allow dough to rest for 10 minutes. Preheat oven to 220°C/425°F/Gas 7. Turn dough on to a well-floured surface and knead for about 4 minutes. Shape into 2 rounds or 2 tins, brush with olive oil, dust with flour and allow to prove for a further 20 minutes. Lower oven temperature to 200°C/400°F/Gas 6 and bake for 35 minutes. Remove from oven and allow to cool on a wire rack.

Roly's Birthday Cake

Serves 4

1 x chocolate sponge (see recipe)
1 x dark truffle mousse (see recipe)
150 ml stock syrup (see page 128)
2 measures Cointreau
100 ml double cream, freshly whipped
25 g dark chocolate, for decoration
200 g white chocolate
selection of fruits in season: strawberries,
redcurrants, Chinese lanterns etc.

Chocolate Sponge
8 eggs
240 g caster sugar
120 g cream flour, sifted
60 g drinking chocolate
60 g cocoa powder
1 teaspoon vanilla essence

Truffle Mousse
400 g dark Belgian chocolate
600 ml double cream
2 whole eggs
1 measure Cointreau

Preheat oven to 200°C/400°F/Gas 6. Line a 20.5 cm cake tin with parchment paper and grease well. In a mixing bowl, whisk the sugar and eggs together until pale and fluffy — about 10 minutes on the highest speed of an electric mixer. In another bowl, sieve the cocoa, drinking chocolate and flour together. Add the essence to the egg mixture and turn off the mixer. Sift the flour mix on to the egg mixture and fold in very gently until it reaches a chocolate batter consistency. Pour this into the tin and bake until the sponge is set and fully risen — about 30–35 minutes. Remove from oven, turn out on to a wire rack to cool. When cool, cut the sponge crossways into 4 separate rounds.

To make the Truffle Mousse: Boil a small pot of water and melt the chocolate in a bowl over the water, making sure no water comes in contact with the chocolate. Remove chocolate and set aside. Semi-whip the cream. In another bowl, whisk the eggs vigorously over the hot water for about one minute. Remove from heat and continue to whisk the eggs until they have cooled and are light and fluffy. Pour the alcohol on to the eggs and fold in. Now add the chocolate to the egg and continue to fold. Finally, fold in the cream until a rich mousse is formed.

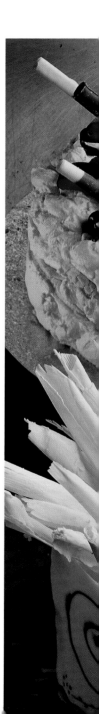

Roly's Birthday Cake

To assemble the Birthday Cake: Line a 20.5 cm tin with cling film leaving some hanging over the edges. Place one round of sponge at the bottom and soak with stock syrup. Cover the sponge with some mousse and layer the cake this way until you reach the top of the tin. Finish with a layer of sponge and place in fridge for 24 hours. Melt the chocolate for decoration in separate bowls and set aside. Place a 10 cm sheet of greaseproof paper on the table and, using a piping bag filled with melted dark chocolate, pipe whatever decorations you want in dark chocolate on to the paper. Put this in the fridge and when the chocolate is set on the paper, remove and put back on the table. Now pour over the melted white chocolate and using a palette knife spread from one end to the other until fully covered. Transfer to fridge to set. When set, remove cake from the tin and place on to a cake board. Remove cling film, wrap the chocolate band around the cake and replace in the fridge for 10 minutes. Finally, peel the paper from the chocolate. Fill centre with cream and decorate with fruit.

Tip: Any leftover melted chocolate can be spread on to a worktop and using a scraper made into chocolate curl. Spread chocolate very thinly using a palette knife and allow to set before scraping.

25

Warm Strawberry and Plum Crêpes

Makes 10–12 crêpes

Crêpes

250 g gluten-free flour
55 g caster sugar
4 whole eggs
650 ml milk
200 ml cream
1 teaspoon vanilla essence
pinch of salt

Strawberry and Plum Compote

1 punnet fresh strawberries
6 fresh plums
100 ml water
50 g sugar
1 orange zest and juice
ground ginger

Sift the flour and salt together in a bowl. Add the eggs and mix into the flour. Gradually add in milk and cream, making sure no lumps form. (If they do, pass the mixture through a sieve.) Finally, add essence or flavouring. To cook, heat a lightly oiled non-stick pan and pour in enough mixture to cover the base — not too thick. When one side is cooked, flip over and repeat on the other side. When crêpe is finished, place it on to some greaseproof paper.

To make the Strawberry and Plum Compote:
Wash all fruit and cut into quarters, removing stones from plums. Bring water, sugar, orange juice and zest to the boil in a pot, add plums and cook until just soft. Place the compote to one side and allow to cool until the mix is warm. Now add strawberries.

To serve, pour compote over crêpes, add a large scoop of double cream and dredge with icing sugar.

Gluten-Free Breads

Makes 3 x 450 g mixes
1 kg white flour, gluten-free
800 ml tepid water
2 sachets yeast
80 g butter, melted
2 egg yolks
1 teaspoon salt
20 g sugar

Basic White Dough
Place flour, sugar and salt in a bowl. Mix the yeast in with the water until it is fully dissolved. (It is important not to have the water over 40°C as it will destroy the yeast.) Mix on speed 1 of a mixer for about one minute, gradually adding in the butter and the eggs until it forms a smooth batter. Divide the mix into 3 separate batches to make 3 kinds of bread.

1 x batch white dough
75 g tomato purée
20 g sun-dried tomatoes, chopped
15 g fennel seeds

Tomato and Fennel Bread
Heat oven to 200°C/400°F/Gas 6. Mix all ingredients together until you have a reddish batter. If it is very runny, whisk in more flour. Place in a 450 g bread tin and leave to prove for 40 minutes in a warm place. If you cover the tin with cling film, it will prove more quickly. When proved, remove cling film, brush with egg yolk or oil and bake for 30–35 minutes.

1 x batch white dough
75 g cooked bacon, chopped
75 g onion (baked to remove moisture)
1 clove garlic, crushed (optional)

Bacon and Onion Bread
Make this bread the same way as the tomato and fennel, but make sure the onion and bacon are chopped into bite-sized pieces.

1 x batch white dough
150 g fresh herbs (parsley, basil) or
3 tablespoons pesto
2 cloves garlic
10 ml olive oil
30 g Parmesan cheese, powdered

Pesto/Herb Bread
In a food processor, whizz the herbs, garlic oil and Parmesan until puréed. Hand whisk this mixture through the white dough and bake as for tomato and fennel bread. Commercially made pesto in jars adds excellent flavour to the bread.

Spring

Starters

Asparagus and Goat's Cheese Tart

Crab Cakes with Sweetcorn Relish

Spring Roll of Root Vegetables, Bamboo Shoots and Water-Chestnuts

Turnip Soup with Turmeric and Cream

Tomato and Mozzarella Tart

Main Courses

Fillet of Beef with Cracked Black Pepper Potato Cake and Brandy Cream

Roast Fillet of Salmon or Trout with Apricot Salsa

Roast Breast of Duck with Grilled Polenta, Creamed Spinach and Duck Jus

Loin of Spring Lamb rolled in Herbs and Pastry with Fondant Potatoes and
   Ratatouille-filled Courgette Baskets

Roast Curried Sea Bass with Girolles, Confit of Garlic and Sauternes Sauce

Roast Stuffed Fillets of Pork in Rhubarb and Ginger Sauce

Desserts

Honey and Poppy-Seed Parfait with Peanut Tuilles

White Chocolate and Fresh Fruit Pavlova with Lemon Curd

Mango Syllabub with Poached Apricots

Melon, Vodka and Orange Jelly

Nature determines the terms of our cooking and dictates the produce we use; we change our menu four times a year at the beginning of each season. In spring tulips or daffodils decorate the tables and the place looks clean and bright. Cold and warm water fish come on the market at the end of January when you start to notice the change. March and April bring spring lamb, wild salmon, baby vegetables, more small things like sugar snap peas, baby beet, asparagus, and new potatoes from France and Italy building up to meet the Irish supplies. While our regular favourites like chicken and beef appear on the menu, this is the time for succulent racks of lamb which we buy from Oughterard in Galway straight off the mountains. They are put on the train from Galway and we pick them up in Dublin.

Our cooking lightens up a lot in spring and sauces are lighter too. I think of salmon with apricot salsa, lamb with herbs, fresh asparagus tarts. Our customers are simple eaters who like food they associate with their own lives such as potato and leek soup, for example, a staple dish. At this time of year we are more inclined to poach salmon than pan-fry it and we make more salads than buttered or roasted vegetables. For desserts, people love pavlovas and chocolate roulades, but white and dark chocolate mousses as well as tarts are also popular.

The rugby season is a big social event in Dublin and brings Welsh, Scottish, English, French and now Italian visitors; with Lansdowne Road on our doorstep, home games are always lively occasions. Friends who only meet up once a year for the Triple Crown (now the Six Nations) look for their regular tables — it's like a big party that starts on Wednesday and continues until Sunday lunch time. This brings a big demand for sirloin and fillet steaks; our beef comes from Kilkenny and is top quality. The home team, who occasionally eat at the restaurant before the match, are fortified for the game by our big bowls of pasta!

The first European tourists start arriving at this time and American contingents descend around St Patrick's Day. I like to keep the menu Irish, but like Old Masters I draw a lot of inspiration from classical cuisine for dishes like fillet of pork with rhubarb, a popular main course that goes well with a Gewurtztraminer. Our pork comes from Meath and is excellent.

In the markets, which we visit from time to time to touch base with our suppliers, it's a real sign of spring when the first of the local produce starts to appear. It's the time of the year when we get to meet the farmer from whom we buy our asparagus, for example. All the producers we deal with are special because, like us, they take pride in their product.

Asparagus and Goat's Cheese Tart

Serves 8

20 g unsalted butter
1 onion, peeled and finely chopped
400 g cooked asparagus
100 g firm goat's cheese
3 eggs
150 ml double cream
1 x 25.5 cm pastry tart case (see recipe)

Pastry Case
1 egg yolk
120 g plain flour
50 g unsalted butter
45 g cream cheese
1 teaspoon lemon juice

To make the Pastry Case: Heat oven to 200°C/400°F/Gas 6. Sift flour into a bowl and add salt. Rub in the butter and cream cheese until well incorporated. Add the egg yolk, lemon juice and one teaspoon of iced water and mix to a smooth dough. Roll out pastry on a lightly floured surface and line a 25.5 cm loose bottomed flan tin. Cut a circle of greaseproof paper to fit the pastry base and weight with dried beans. Bake for 15 minutes, remove beans and paper and return to oven for a further 5 minutes. Remove and set aside.

Reduce heat to 180°C/350°F/Gas 4. Melt the butter in a small pan and cook the onion until soft, stirring frequently. Remove from the heat and leave to cool. Cut the asparagus spears in half, keeping the spear heads intact, then cut the rest into small rounds. Spread the onion over the hot pastry case, then add the crumbled cheese and the asparagus rounds. Whisk the eggs and cream together, pour into the pastry case and bake for 15 minutes. Arrange the asparagus spears on top and bake for a further 25–30 minutes until set.

Asparagus and Goat's Cheese Tart

Crab Cakes with Sweetcorn Relish

Serves 4

50 g mayonnaise
200 g cooked white crabmeat
100 g poached white fish,
e.g. haddock or cod
4 spring onions, finely chopped
4 gherkins, finely chopped
100 g plain mashed potato
sweetcorn relish (see recipe)
100 g white breadcrumbs
100 g plain flour } for coating
2 eggs, beaten

Check the crabmeat carefully, removing any pieces of shell. Mix all the ingredients together and season with salt and pepper. Form the mixture into 8 cakes. Coat the cakes in flour, then in the beaten egg and finally in the breadcrumbs. Heat some oil in a heavy based frying pan and fry the cakes on a medium heat for 3–4 minutes on both sides until golden brown and warmed through.

Sweetcorn Relish
2 corn on the cob, cooked
4 tablespoons caster sugar
juice of 1 lemon
2 tablespoons red wine vinegar
1 red onion, peeled and finely chopped
1 red pepper, skinned, deseeded and finely diced
1 tablespoon olive oil

To make Sweetcorn Relish: With a small, sharp knife, cut the kernels from the corn cobs. Put the sugar, lemon juice and vinegar in a small saucepan and bring to the boil. Remove from heat and leave to cool. Mix the corn, onion and peppers with the olive oil, stir into the cooled liquid and season to taste.

Serve with a little salad and the sweetcorn relish on the side.

Spring Roll of Root Vegetables, Bamboo Shoots and Water-Chestnuts

Serves 4

4 sheets spring roll pastry
1 carrot, finely sliced
1 leek, finely sliced
1 onion, finely sliced
1 packet bamboo shoots
½ tin water-chestnuts
¼ chilli
2 cloves garlic, finely chopped
1 teaspoon Chinese five spice
1 teaspoon paprika
10 ml soy sauce
10 g ginger, finely chopped
1 drop Tabasco sauce

In a heavy saucepan, fry carrot, leek and onion until they become limp. Add ginger and garlic, but do not overcook as garlic will become bitter. Slice up water-chestnuts and add to your mix, cooking continuously on a low heat. Finally, add bamboo shoots, chilli, spices, soy sauce and Tabasco. Remove from heat, strain all the juices and allow to cool. Season to taste.

Take one sheet of spring roll pastry and brush with beaten egg. Place one portion (about 50 g of mix) in the middle of the pastry and begin to roll to the other side, folding in the sides as you go. Continue until you have 4 rolls. Deep fry in a preheated fryer until pastry crisps.

Serve with a lightly tossed green salad.

Turnip Soup with Turmeric and Cream

Serves 8

25 g butter
500 g fresh turnip, cubed
1 large onion, chopped
1 white of leek, chopped
1 large carrot, sliced
100 g peeled potato, diced
1 litre + 200 ml chicken/vegetable stock
(see pages 126/127)
500 ml double cream
2 teaspoons turmeric
1 sprig thyme
1 bay leaf
salt and pepper

In a large saucepan, sauté the onion and leek in butter over a low heat without colouring them, then add thyme, bay leaf and turmeric and stir. Add the litre of stock, carrot, turnip and raw potatoes and bring to the boil. Simmer for about 15 minutes until turnip is fully cooked and then stir in the cream. Remove from the heat, discard bay leaf, liquidise in a blender, add remaining hot stock and strain through a sieve. Season with salt and pepper.

Tip: For a stronger colour add more carrots.

Serve the soup with a generous topping of freshly whisked cream.

Tomato and Mozzarella Tart

Tomato and Mozzarella Tart

Serves 4

2 packets Buffalo mozzarella cheese
4 plum tomatoes
16 basil leaves
basil pesto
(see recipe on page 128)
olive oil to taste
salt and pepper
½ pack Jus Roll puff pastry
(cut in 13 cm rounds for bases)

First pre-cook the puff pastry bases in the oven at 200°C/400°F/Gas 6 for 15 minutes until brown. When cool, place on a baking tray and place another baking tray on top to prevent the pastry rising.

Slice the plum tomatoes and mozzarella cheese finely. Place first the tomato then the cheese slices around the base, then add the 4 basil leaves. Drizzle olive oil on top of the tart. Season with salt and pepper. Place in the oven at 180°F/350°C/Gas 4 for 15 minutes or until cooked. Remove from the oven, place on a plate and garnish with basil pesto.

Fillet of Beef with Cracked Black Pepper Potato Cake and Brandy Cream

Serves 4

4 thick fillets of beef
1 tablespoon brandy

Potato Cakes
225 g potatoes, freshly boiled
2 teaspoons cracked black pepper
1 egg yolk
½ teaspoon salt
35 g spring onions
50 g flour
25 g butter

Brandy Cream
2 tablespoons brandy
150 ml double cream
100 ml beef stock or jus
(see page 125)

For the Potato Cakes: Mash the freshly cooked potatoes, add salt, melted butter, cracked peppers, spring onions, egg yolk and flour and mix together into a dough. Roll out into 4 circular shapes 6 mm thick. Brown on both sides on a hot, slightly greased pan until cooked.

For the Beef Fillets: Place fillets in a hot frying pan with some butter, salt and pepper. Cook on both sides until nice and pink in the centre. Remove fillets, deglaze the pan with the brandy, then add jus and reduce by half. Add brandy and cream, reduce to sauce consistency and season to taste.

To serve, place fillets on a plate, top with the potato cake and pour the brandy cream around the steak. Garnish with a sprig of watercress.

Fillet of Beef with Cracked Black Pepper Potato Cake and Brandy Cream

Roast Fillet of Salmon or Trout with Apricot Salsa

Serves 4

4 x 125 g fillets salmon or trout
50 g dried apricots, diced
50 g cucumber, diced
1 red onion, diced
1 red chilli, diced
1 plum tomato, chopped
1 teaspoon sugar, warmed with
2 teaspoons vinegar
juice of 1 lime
olive oil
salt and pepper

Heat oven to 200°C/400°F/Gas 6. Season the salmon with salt and pepper. Heat a small amount of olive oil in a frying pan and seal the salmon on both sides until golden brown. Transfer to a baking tray and cook in the oven for 10 minutes approximately. To make the salsa, mix all the ingredients together, adding the vinegar and sugar at the end, then season to taste.

To serve, divide the salsa between 4 plates and place the cooked salmon on top.

Roast Fillet of Salmon or Trout with Apricot Salsa

Roast Breast of Duck with Grilled Polenta, Creamed Spinach and Duck Jus

Preparation for this recipe needs to be started a day beforehand.

Serves 4

4 portions polenta (see recipe)
4 duck breasts
4 portions creamed spinach (see recipe)
400 ml duck jus (see recipe)

Polenta
100 g polenta
200 ml chicken stock (see page 126)
25 g Parmesan cheese, grated
15 g butter
6 sage leaves, chopped

Duck Jus *(makes ½ litre approx.)*
bones from two ducks, chopped
250 g onion, chopped
250 g carrots, chopped
100 g celery, chopped
1 clove garlic
50 g tomato purée
1 small bunch thyme
1½ litres chicken stock (see page 126)

To cook Polenta: Bring the chicken stock to the boil in a saucepan, stir in the polenta and cook over a low heat for 2–3 minutes, stirring constantly. It will thicken quickly. Stir in the Parmesan cheese, butter and chopped sage and then spread the mixture evenly into a 2.5 cm deep buttered tray or dish. Leave to set overnight. Turn the polenta on to a chopping board and using a 5 cm diameter pastry cutter cut out 4 rounds.

To make Duck Jus: Heat oven to 200°C/400°F/Gas 6 and roast duck bones for about 30 minutes until nicely browned, then add vegetables and roast for another 10 minutes. Transfer the bones and the vegetables to a large saucepan and cover with chicken stock. Bring to the boil, skim off any fat or scum, then add the tomato purée and thyme and simmer for 2 hours, skimming frequently. Strain through a colander then through a fine sieve, return to the saucepan and reduce by half to concentrate the flavour. Any leftover jus can be frozen.

Heat oven to 200°C/400°F/Gas 6. Season the duck breasts with salt and pepper and seal both sides in vegetable oil in a very hot pan. Transfer duck breasts on to a hot roasting tray skin side down and roast in the oven for 8–10 minutes. Remove from oven and leave to rest for 2–3 minutes. The polenta can be heated on the same tray as the duck; it will also take 8–10 minutes and should be turned halfway through so both sides are crispy.

Creamed Spinach

100 g spinach purée (buy frozen spinach)
100 ml cream
pinch of nutmeg
½ an onion, finely diced
15 g butter

To make Creamed Spinach: Melt the butter in a small saucepan, then add the onions and cook without browning until soft. Add cream and reduce by half. Put the defrosted spinach in a clean tea towel, squeeze to remove excess water and add to the cream with the nutmeg and stir. Season to taste.

To serve, carve the duck into small slices, put the polenta topped with the warm creamed spinach in the centre of the 4 plates and arrange duck slices around it. Spoon over the duck jus.

Loin of Spring Lamb rolled in Herbs and Pastry with Fondant Potatoes and Ratatouille-filled Courgette Baskets

Serves 4

4 x 150 g pieces loin of lamb
4 sheets spring roll pastry
1 teaspoon each chopped tarragon,
parsley and coriander
4 courgette baskets (see recipe)
4 portions lamb sauce (see page 127)

Fondant Potatoes
4 medium potatoes
100 g unsalted butter, diced
100 ml water approx.
1 clove garlic, cut in 3

Courgette Baskets filled with Ratatouille
4 medium courgettes
1 red pepper, finely diced
1 yellow pepper, finely diced
½ an aubergine, finely diced
1 onion, finely diced
2 cloves garlic, crushed
1 teaspoon tomato purée
2 tomatoes, finely chopped
100 ml olive oil
100 g Parmesan cheese
salt and pepper

Preheat oven to 220°C/425°F/Gas 7. In a hot pan seal the lamb loins in a little oil. Season with salt and pepper and roll in herbs. Lay the spring roll pastry out flat and brush the edge with egg wash. Put the lamb in the centre, fold in the two sides, then roll. Cook the lamb in a hot oven for 15 minutes.

To make Fondant Potatoes: Peel and square off each potato. Using a 5 cm plain round cutter, cut a shape out of each potato. Put the butter, potatoes and garlic in a small frying pan, add water and season with salt and pepper. Cook on a slow heat for about 15 minutes each side until the potatoes are golden brown.

To make Courgette Baskets: Preheat oven to 200°C/400°F/Gas 6. Top and tail the courgettes and cut lengthways, removing the core with a small knife or Parisienne scoop. Cook in boiling salted water for 5 minutes, refresh in iced water and set aside. Heat the oil in a pot, add the onion and garlic and cook slowly for 5 minutes. Add peppers and cook for a further 5 minutes. Add the aubergine, cook for 5 more minutes, then the tomatoes and tomato purée and cook for 5–10 minutes more. Season with salt and pepper. Fill the courgettes with the ratatouille, sprinkle with Parmesan and bake for 15–20 minutes.

To serve, cut lamb in half, put at the front of a large plate with the fondant potato and courgette basket at the back. Spoon sauce around it.

Loin of Spring Lamb rolled in Herbs and Pastry with Fondant Potatoes and Ratatouille-filled Courgette Baskets

45

Roast Curried Sea Bass with Girolles, Confit of Garlic and Sauternes Sauce

Serves 4

4 x 150 g pieces sea bass
120 ml olive oil
25 g curry powder
36 sprigs thyme
150 g small girolles
25 g unsalted butter
20 cloves confit of garlic (see recipe)
Sauternes sauce (see recipe)

Confit of Garlic
20 cloves garlic, peeled
25 g unsalted butter

Sauternes Sauce
4 shallots, peeled and finely diced
100 g unsalted butter
150 ml Sauternes
100 ml chicken stock (see page 126)
100 ml fish stock (see page 126)
150 ml double cream

To make Confit of Garlic: Put the garlic in a small pan of cold water, bring to the boil and boil for 30 seconds. Drain and repeat this blanching two more times. To serve, crisp up in a frying pan with the butter or some olive oil.

To make Sauternes Sauce: Sweat the shallots in 25 g of butter until soft but not coloured. Add Sauternes and boil to reduce by half. Do the same with the fish stock and chicken stock. Add the cream and simmer for 2 minutes, pass through a fine sieve into a clean saucepan and return to the heat. Dice the remaining butter and whisk into the sauce. Do not let it boil.

Deep fry the sprigs of thyme in hot oil for a few seconds and drain on some kitchen paper. Mix 50 ml of the olive oil and the curry powder to make a thin paste. Brush this all over the sea bass. Preheat a non-stick pan and cook the sea bass in the remaining olive oil for 5–6 minutes depending on thickness. In a separate pan, pan-fry the girolles for 5–6 minutes in the butter and when almost cooked add the confit of garlic. Heat the sauce through gently.

To serve, place the sea bass in the centre of the plate and arrange the girolles, garlic and thyme neatly over and around. Spoon the sauce around.

Roast Stuffed Fillets of Pork in Rhubarb and Ginger Sauce

Serves 4

2 fillets pork 325–400 g each
175 g butter
275 ml cider
225 g white breadcrumbs
2 onions, chopped
parsley and thyme, chopped
3 sticks rhubarb
1 small piece root ginger, grated (14 g)
seasoning
watercress for garnish

Preheat oven to 220°C/425°F/Gas 7. Slice fillets of pork down the middle lengthways without cutting all the way through. Open out and beat flat with a mallet or the side of a cleaver. For the stuffing, fry one chopped onion, thyme, parsley and one stick of rhubarb finely diced in half the butter and mix in the breadcrumbs and seasoning. Cover the centre of the flattened pork with the stuffing and roll up tying with string. With the rest of the butter melted on a roasting tray put in pork and cook in the oven for approximately 30 minutes. When cooked, cut into 4 portions and keep hot. Empty the fat from the roasting tray and add some chopped rhubarb, onion, ginger and finally the cider. Bring to the boil and reduce by half. Strain and pour over meat.

Serve garnished with some blanched rhubarb and watercress.

Honey and Poppy-Seed Parfait with Peanut Tuilles

A delicate, frozen dessert, lighter than ice-cream.

Serves 8

Parfait

4 egg yolks
100 g honey
½ litre double cream, semi-whipped
1 vanilla pod, split and scraped
poppy-seeds

Peanut Tuilles

110 g caster sugar
130 g soft flour
130 g butter
130 g egg-white
vanilla essence
100 g peanuts, finely chopped

To make the Parfait: Prepare moulds or small loaf tins and line with cling film. Whip egg yolks at high speed on a machine until pale. In a heavy pot, boil honey to 116°C/240°F on a sugar thermometer (softball). Pour cooked honey slowly on to the whipped egg yolks and turn machine on full again. Whisk until cold (feel bottom of the bowl) which might take 10–15 minutes. Fold in semi-whipped cream to the egg mixture and add as many poppy-seeds as preferred. Pour into mould, cover well and freeze overnight.

To make Peanut Tuilles: Preheat oven to 190°C/375°F/Gas 5. Cream butter, sugar and egg-white, then blend in flour until you have a pliable paste. Spread into a wafer stencil shaped on a clean greased tray or silicone mat (can be found in any catering supply shop) and sprinkle with nuts. Bake for approximately 3–4 minutes until the edges become golden. Remove from oven and shape immediately.

To serve, cut a slice of parfait with a hot knife, place in between 2 wafers and drizzle with honey and fresh cream.

White Chocolate and Fresh Fruit Pavlova with Lemon Curd

Serves 8

3 clean egg-whites
175 g caster sugar, divide in half
1 teaspoon cornflour, sifted
1 teaspoon white vinegar
½ teaspoon vanilla essence

Pavlova filling
150 ml double cream
150 ml lemon curd
225 g mixed summer fruits (mango, papaya, kiwi, strawberry, redcurrants, Chinese lantern and passion fruits)

Lemon Curd (makes about 375 g)
3 lemons (grated rind and juice)
2 eggs, slightly beaten
50 g butter
225 g caster sugar

To make the Pavlova: Heat oven to 130°C/250°C/Gas ½. Line 2 baking sheets with non-stick baking parchment. In a very clean bowl, whisk egg-whites with the vinegar on the highest speed until they form stiff peaks, adding the first half of the sugar. Whisk on full speed for about one minute, then stop. Mix the other half of the sugar with the cornflour and fold very carefully into the stiff whites using a spatula, taking care not to knock the air out of the mix. Vanilla essence can be added now. Pipe into small discs on the prepared baking sheets using a plain nozzle. Cook for approximately 55 minutes or until the meringues lift off the paper. Allow to cool before decorating. At this stage the meringue will probably crack and sink a little. It should be mallowy in the centre.

Tip: Always leave door slightly ajar when cooking Pavlova, as steam will cause it to collapse.

To make Lemon Curd: Put all the ingredients into the top of a double saucepan or in a basin standing in a pan of simmering water. Stir until sugar has dissolved. Continue heating, stirring from time to time until the curd thickens. Strain using a fine sieve and allow to cool in refrigerator until needed.

Assembly of Pavlova: Prepare the fresh fruits into small, enticing pieces. Start with a disc at the bottom, place a spoonful of cream on top of the disc and arrange fruits. Continue this once more until you have a tower effect with heavy fruits on the bottom and lighter fruits on the top layer. Finish by scraping the passion fruits over the top. Hold on to the shells and fill with lemon curd for an attractive garnish. Decorate with white chocolate shavings and dust liberally with icing sugar.

49

Mango Syllabub with Poached Apricots

Serves 6

60 g caster sugar
175 ml Muscat dessert wine
700 g ripe apricots, stoned and halved
100 ml mango purée
500 ml double cream
2 rosemary sprigs
1 vanilla pod, scraped

Put the sugar and wine in a saucepan and heat gently until the sugar dissolves. Add apricots and simmer until soft — about 5 minutes. Strain the apricots, retaining the juice. In another pot, heat 200 ml of the cream, rosemary and vanilla pod gently to boiling point. Remove from heat and leave to infuse for 30 minutes. Take 6 tall glasses and spoon in the apricots. Remove rosemary and vanilla pod from the cream, add remaining cream, mango purée and 200 ml of poaching syrup and whip until the mix is thick and makes a figure of eight. Pour the mix over the apricots and chill for 2½–3 hours.

Serve with boudoir biscuits or chocolate shavings.

Melon, Vodka and Orange Jelly

A fresh and tangy dessert that clears the palate

Serves 10

375 ml fresh orange juice, strained
125 ml stock syrup (see page 128)
70 ml fresh mango, crushed
3 oranges
2 dashes vodka
dash lemon juice
6 leaves gelatine
selection of 3 varieties of melon:
cantaloupe, ogen and watermelon

Soak the gelatine in cold water until soft. Remove from water and dissolve in a bowl over a pot of hot water. Add the vodka. In another bowl, mix the orange juice, mango and stock syrup. Segment oranges and finely dice melons, retaining some for decoration. Mix in with the liquid and add the gelatine to the orange mix while the gelatine is still warm. Pour the prepared jelly into moulds and set in the fridge for 12–24 hours. Unmould by immersing in hot water. Cups or glasses can be used instead of pudding moulds.

To serve, surround with seasonal berries.

Melon, Vodka and Orange Jelly

Summer

Starters

Chicken Tandoori Terrine with Yoghurt Riata and Poppadums

Melon Marinated in Passion Fruit, Brandy and Ginger

Cashel Blue Cheese and Roast Tomato Bruschetta with Tomato and Apple Chutney

Avocado, Tomato, Crab and Smoked Salmon Parcel, Rocket Salad and Shallot Dressing

Main Courses

Dublin Bay Prawns with Garlic, Chilli and Ginger Butter, Coriander-scented Wild Rice

Roast Fillet of Monkfish with Roasted Peppers, Balsamic Vinegar and Olive Oil Dressing

Baked Fillet of Plaice stuffed with Crab, and Carrot and Tarragon Butter

Pea Risotto with Feta Cheese and Rocket

Roast Breast of Chicken with Coriander Creamed Potato and Lemongrass-scented
  Vegetable Broth

Fried Veal Livers with Buttered Savoy Cabbage and Madeira Jus

Desserts

Roly's Summer Pudding with Fresh Berries

Strawberries with Black Pepper Sable and Gratinated Champagne Sabayon

Clementine Gratin with Sabayon of Cointreau

Caramelised Orange Shortbread Tartlet

Chocolate Fig Brownies with Frozen Raspberry Pâté

In summer when it's sunny the sun will shine right into the kitchens all day long. That light and freshness is reflected in the menu. It's a time of year when many of our regular customers go on holiday. We get early evening diners from local guest houses and hotels. Many people out walking and thinking about their weight will drop into the restaurant for a main course only. A husband will meet his wife for a meal and then go to the theatre, or take a stroll in Herbert Park before coming in to dinner. The atmosphere is more casual. Herbert Park, one of the oldest and most popular parks in Dublin, is where I go every morning when I get up, whatever the weather. It's a restful oasis on our doorstep and in July and August we can hear the strains of the lunchtime band performances through the open windows of the restaurant.

At this time of year people drink more water than wine at lunch and choose lighter fare. There are all sorts of social events during the season, in particular the Horse Show in August at the Royal Dublin Society (RDS) beside us; on Ladies' Day, our rooms are filled with elegant women wearing hats. People dine either before or after a concert at the Point; and on Bloomsday, 16 June, Joyce aficionados come in dressed up in straw boaters and Edwardian stripes to celebrate that immortal day in *Ulysses*.

Risottos and veal liver, which we serve with Savoy cabbage and Madeira jus, are popular in summer. It's the time of year when Irish produce is at its best and people tend to eat more fish like cod, monkfish or skate and order more side salads. Though we serve prawns all year round — we buy 18 kg a day — they are at their best around this time. We serve them with garlic, chilli and ginger butter which is fresh and summery. Crab and smoked salmon parcels, cheese and roast tomato bruschettas will go on the starter menu.

We are constantly trying different types of potatoes and recipes like *pommes de terre fondantes*, but good mashed potatoes (usually with Roosters) and roast potatoes (Dells) are always in demand. In 1998 we put fish and chips with mushy peas on the menu to surprise customers and it was an instant success. The haddock is deep fried in a delicious beer batter and the chips presented in cones of waxed newspaper which are specially made for us so the print doesn't run. (For recipe see page 112.)

Nothing is more summery than strawberries and occasionally we serve them with pepper and lemon — a squeeze of lemon gives them sharpness while the mustiness of the pepper accentuates the scent of the freshly picked fruit. Simple touches like that enhance the natural flavour of quality ingredients. Until recently, my sister Gemma used to grow all the strawberries in her own hothouse in County Meath, as well as herbs and baby vegetables.

Chicken Tandoori Terrine with Yoghurt Riata and Poppadums

Make this a day in advance; it takes a bit of effort, but it is amply rewarded!
Serves 8

6 chicken fillets, skinned and boned
5 red peppers
20 large spinach leaves
½ bunch basil leaves
Tabasco sauce
½ kg ghee (Indian clarified butter)*
*You can use clarified butter instead of ghee, but the flavour will not be the same.

Tandoori Marinade
200 g tandoori paste
200 g Greek yoghurt
1 teaspoon mace
1 teaspoon nutmeg
1 teaspoon cumin powder
1 teaspoon ginger
1 teaspoon paprika
1 tablespoon cochineal
1 tablespoon tomato purée
juice of a lemon

Score the chicken. Mix all the ingredients for the marinade together. Rub the marinade into the chicken breasts really well and leave in the marinade overnight. Heat oven to 200°C/400°F/Gas 6. Drop spinach leaves into boiling water for 10 seconds and refresh in iced water. Pat them dry. Melt the ghee. Place the chickens on a wire rack, baste with ghee and put wire rack on a tray in the oven and cook for about 35 minutes, basting every 10 minutes. Remove and put peppers on the same tray and cook until skin is wrinkly and easy to take off — about 15 minutes. Line the terrine mould with oil, then cling film, letting it hang over the edge. Brush cling film with ghee butter. Cover the mould with dry spinach, making sure not to leave any gaps and let the spinach hang over the mould.

Chicken Tandoori Terrine with Yoghurt Riata and Poppadums

Riata

25 g cucumber, diced
25 g walnuts, chopped
25 g mint, chopped
½ teaspoon cumin seeds
½ teaspoon cayenne powder
150 g Greek yoghurt

To assemble the Terrine: Start with a layer of skinned and deseeded peppers, then brush with melted ghee, followed by a layer of basil, then season and sprinkle with Tabasco. Now add a layer of chicken and brush with ghee. Repeat this 3 times. Fold spinach over the last layer and brush with ghee, again leaving no gaps. Fold cling film over the terrine. Cover the mould in tin foil and pierce small holes into the terrine with a fork. Place an empty terrine mould on top of the chicken one and put a weight on top of it. Leave overnight in a fridge. Mix all the ingredients for the riata together and season to taste.

Remove terrine from the mould and cling film. Place it on a roll of cling film. Get someone to hold the other end of the cling film and roll the terrine tightly. Tie each end of the terrine with string. Slice terrine into thick pieces and remove the cling film.

Serve with riata and poppadums.

Melon Marinated in Passion Fruit, Brandy and Ginger

Serves 4

1 melon (cantaloupe/ogen or half of each)
2 passion fruit
2 large oranges
1 shot brandy
25 g root ginger, grated
4 sprigs mint

Using a Parisienne scoop, make melon balls. Squeeze oranges and blend juice with grated ginger in a blender. Strain into a bowl, add brandy and scoop in the passion fruit. Marinate the melon balls in this mixture overnight.

Serve melon in a bowl, spoon over marinade and garnish with a sprig of mint.

Cashel Blue Cheese and Roast Tomato Bruschetta with Tomato and Apple Chutney

Serves 4

4 slices Cashel blue cheese
4 tomatoes, cut in half
4 thick slices tomato and fennel bread
(see page 27)
6–8 tablespoons pesto (see page 128)

Chutney
1 onion, chopped
4 tomatoes, chopped
1 red pepper, deseeded and chopped
5 tablespoons white wine vinegar
5 tablespoons sugar
½ teaspoon chopped chilli
½ teaspoon chopped ginger
1 tablespoon tomato purée
1 can tomatoes (strained)
2 large eating apples, peeled

Brush bread with pesto on each side and reserve. Sprinkle tomatoes with a little salt, sugar and some olive oil and roast them in the oven for 45 minutes at 130°C/250°F/Gas ½. Grill bread on each side until lightly toasted and place 2 halves of the roasted tomatoes on the bread and a slice of cheese on each. Drizzle remaining pesto over each bruschetta and place in the oven at 180°C/350°F/Gas 4 for about 7 minutes.

To make the Chutney: Into a mixer put onions, tomatoes, pepper, vinegar, sugar, chilli, ginger and tomato purée and blend together. Place mixture in a pot, add strained tomatoes and simmer for about 30–40 minutes. Chop apples into big cubes and add to the chutney, then simmer for another 5 minutes.

Serve the bruschetta with chutney and salad leaves.

Avocado, Tomato, Crab and Smoked Salmon Parcel, Rocket Salad and Shallot Dressing

Serves 4

8 slices smoked salmon
140 g white crab, picked
1 large avocado
2 tomatoes, chopped (plunge in boiling water for just under a minute, skin, deseed and chop)
juice of ½ a lemon
1 tablespoon Greek yoghurt
salt and pepper

Shallot Dressing

2 tablespoons extra virgin olive oil
2 tablespoons sunflower oil
1 tablespoon capers
1 tablespoon diced shallots
1 tablespoon lemon juice
1 teaspoon sugar
1 teaspoon salt

About 20 rocket leaves

Peel the avocado and dice into small cubes. Squeeze lemon juice over avocado, season with salt and pepper and set aside. Add Greek yoghurt and tomatoes to the picked crab and season. On a small sheet of greaseproof paper, place 2 slices of smoked salmon, overlapping with smooth edges on either side. Put one spoon of avocado and one spoon of crab onto the salmon. Use the paper to roll the salmon over the mix into a cylindrical shape. Mix all the ingredients for the dressing together.

To serve, place salmon on a plate, drizzle dressing around it and place 5 rocket leaves on top of the salmon.

Dublin Bay Prawns with Garlic, Chilli and Ginger Butter, Coriander-scented Wild Rice

Serves 4

700 g prawns, freshly peeled
125 g cooked wild rice
125 g cooked long grain rice
125 g unsalted butter*
15 g chopped garlic*
15 g chopped ginger*
15 g chopped red chilli*
15 g Dijon mustard*
½ teaspoon turmeric*
juice of 1 lemon
50 g chopped coriander
200 ml dry white wine
* denotes butter ingredients

Mix all the butter ingredients together in a blender. Mix the wild and long grain rice together, add coriander and divide the mixture into 4 moulds. Heat half a tablespoon of vegetable oil in a heavy bottomed frying pan until smoking hot, then put in the prawns one by one and cook for 30 seconds each side. Set them aside on to a warm plate. Let the pan cool slightly, then add the butter mixture. When it has melted, return prawns to the pan and add white wine. Season to taste and serve.

Dublin Bay Prawns with Garlic, Chilli and Ginger Butter, Coriander-scented Wild Rice

Roast Fillet of Monkfish with Roasted Peppers, Balsamic Vinegar and Olive Oil Dressing

Serves 4

4 x 150 g fillets monkfish
2 red peppers, deseeded and cut into squares
2 yellow peppers, deseeded and cut into squares
125 g mixed salad leaves
75 ml olive oil
25 ml balsamic vinegar
½ teaspoon Dijon mustard

Heat oven to 240°C/450°F/Gas 8. In an oven-proof dish, mix 50 ml olive oil with the peppers, season with salt and pepper and put in the oven for 15–20 minutes, stirring every 2–3 minutes. To make the dressing, whisk the mustard and vinegar together, season with salt and pepper and slowly add the remaining olive oil. Heat a large frying pan with a small amount of vegetable oil, season monkfish with salt and pepper and place in the pan. When the monkfish is sealed and turning golden brown, reduce heat and turn over the fillets, adding a knob of butter. Cook the monkfish for 6–7 minutes, turning 3–4 times; it will be soft to the touch when cooked.

To serve, layer the peppers and dressed salad leaves on a plate and place monkfish on top.

Baked Fillet of Plaice stuffed with Crab, and Carrot and Tarragon Butter

Serves 4

8 fillets plaice
200 g white crabmeat
1 level tablespoon Dijon mustard
200 ml semi-whipped cream
400 ml carrot and tarragon butter
(see recipe)
100 g breadcrumbs
juice of ½ a lemon

Carrot and Tarragon Butter
100 ml dry white wine
100 ml carrot juice
50 ml white wine vinegar
100 ml cream
50 g unsalted butter
½ teaspoon cracked black pepper
1 small shallot, finely chopped
1 small bunch tarragon, picked and
chopped
2 bay leaves

Heat oven to 200°C/400°F/Gas 6. Mix the mustard and cream together, fold into the crabmeat, then add lemon juice and season with salt and pepper. Place 4 of the plaice fillets on a buttered baking tray and divide the crab mixture between them, smoothing it out with the back of a spoon so that each fillet is covered. Put the remaining 4 fillets on top and season with salt and pepper. Cook in the oven for 15 minutes approximately, remove, sprinkle with breadcrumbs and brown under a preheated grill for about one minute.

To make Carrot and Tarragon Butter: Heat all the ingredients except the cream, butter and tarragon in a small saucepan and reduce by two-thirds. Add cream and boil to reduce by half. Remove bay leaves and slowly whisk in the butter, making sure that the mixture does not boil. Remove from heat and pass through a fine strainer. Season with salt and pepper to taste, then stir in the chopped tarragon.

To serve, put plaice in the centre of a plate and spoon carrot and tarragon butter around it.

Pea Risotto with Feta Cheese and Rocket

Serves 4

*900 ml chicken or vegetable stock
(see pages 126/127)
100 g cooked peas
100 g feta cheese, diced
50 g approx. rocket
1 onion, finely chopped
½ clove garlic, peeled and finely chopped
250 g risotto rice
30 g unsalted butter
salt and pepper
100 ml olive oil*

Bring chicken stock to boiling point, then set aside. Heat the olive oil in a heavy bottomed pan, add the onion and cook until soft, then add garlic and cook for a further 1–2 minutes. Add the rice and cook for about one minute stirring to coat all the grains. Pour in enough stock to cover the rice and cook over a moderate heat, stirring frequently and adding more stock so that the rice is always just covered. It will take about 15–20 minutes for the rice to be fully cooked. At this point add the peas, feta cheese, butter, half the rocket and stir. Season with salt and pepper.

To serve, spoon the risotto into pasta bowls and garnish with the remaining rocket.

Roast Breast of Chicken with Coriander Creamed Potato and Lemongrass-scented Vegetable Broth

Serves 4

4 x 150–225 g chicken breasts
4 portions coriander creamed potato (see recipe)
400 ml chicken stock (see page 126)
1 small head fennel, finely sliced
½ onion, finely diced
1 clove garlic, crushed
1 medium carrot, finely sliced
1 medium courgette, finely sliced
1 stick lemongrass, crushed
6 strands saffron
100 ml olive oil
12 cherry tomatoes
25 g butter

Coriander Creamed Potato

400 g potato, peeled and diced
50 g butter
200 ml double cream
1 tablespoon coriander seeds, crushed
salt and pepper

In a medium-sized, heavy bottomed saucepan, warm the olive oil, add the diced onion, crushed garlic and fennel and cook on a slow heat for approximately 10 minutes. Add chicken stock, crushed lemongrass and saffron and simmer gently for 30 minutes. Remove lemongrass. In a pot of boiling water, blanch the carrot and courgette then refresh in cold water. Season chicken breasts with salt and pepper, put in an oiled oven tray and roast for 25 minutes approximately at 200°C/400°F/Gas 6.

To make Coriander Creamed Potato: Wash potatoes well to remove starch. Place in a saucepan, cover with cold water and add about a teaspoon of salt. Cook the potatoes until they are soft but not mushy, drain well, return to saucepan and dry over a low heat for one minute, stirring so they do not stick. Mash well, add the cream, butter and coriander seeds, mixing with a wooden spoon. Season with salt and pepper to taste.

To serve, warm the coriander creamed potato and divide between 4 bowls. Heat the vegetable broth, adding the carrots, courgettes, cherry tomatoes and butter, stirring constantly until the butter has emulsified.

Roast Breast of Chicken with Coriander Creamed Potato and Lemongrass-scented Vegetable Broth

Fried Veal Livers with Buttered Savoy Cabbage and Madeira Jus

Serves 4

600 g veal liver
20 g plain flour
50 ml oil
150 g unsalted butter
200 ml Madeira
300 ml beef stock (see page 125)
200 g shallots, finely diced
½ clove garlic, crushed
½ head Savoy cabbage, finely shredded
1 teaspoon caraway seeds
1 teaspoon honey

Trim the veal livers and slice thinly into 8 slices, 2 per portion. Season with salt and pepper and dust with flour. Heat the oil and 50 g butter in a saucepan and sauté the liver very quickly on both sides. Remove from the pan and keep warm. Discard fat from the pan, add the Madeira to deglaze and boil to reduce by half. Add beef stock and reduce by half again, then whisk in 50 g butter over a low heat until melted. Strain the sauce into a sauceboat and keep warm.

Buttered Savoy Cabbage

In a heavy bottomed saucepan, melt 50 g butter and fry shallots and garlic in it until transparent and soft. Add Savoy cabbage and cook until soft, then sprinkle in the caraway seeds and stir in the honey.

To serve, arrange cabbage on each plate, place veal livers on top and pour the sauce around each portion.

Roly's Summer Pudding with Fresh Berries

Serves 4–6

225 g raspberries
50 g redcurrants
50 g strawberries
50 g blackcurrants
25 g blackberries
25 g plums
50 g caster sugar
20 ml water
8 large slices white bread or white sponge
25 g unsalted butter, melted

Garnish
fresh fruits
mint
dusting powder

Put the water and sugar in a pot and bring to the boil, then add all the fruits and stew until the juices begin to run. Remove from the heat. Remove the crusts from the bread and cut into triangles. Cut out 6 rounds also for the bottoms of the puddings. Brush 6 individual pudding basins with the melted butter and sprinkle on some caster sugar. Shake upside down to remove excess sugar. Arrange the bread triangles around the sides of the pudding basin, overlapping them at the bottom, so they fit neatly.

Set aside some juice and fruit for decoration. Fill the pudding with the stewed fruit until tightly packed to the top. Cover the bottom with the round of bread. Trim if necessary. Continue with the rest of the puddings as the first. Place a saucer on top of the puddings, then put a 450 g weight on top and refrigerate overnight. To demould the puddings, remove the weight and place the puddings in very hot water for a few seconds. This will melt the butter and it should slide out with a little shake.

To serve, spoon over the juice and decorate the plate with reserved fruits, icing sugar and mint.

Strawberries with Black Pepper Sable and Gratinated Champagne Sabayon

Serves 4

2 punnets fresh strawberries
100 ml cream, freshly whipped

Sable *(makes 10–15 biscuits)*
1 teaspoon vanilla essence
75 g caster sugar
150 g unsalted butter
1 egg
200 g soft flour
35 g ground almonds
2 teaspoons ground black pepper

Champagne Sabayon
75 g sugar
125 g Philadelphia cream cheese
125 ml cream, semi-whisked
4 eggs, separated
1 leaf gelatine
1 glass champagne or white wine

To make the Sable: Heat oven to 190°C/375°F/Gas 5. Cream the butter and sugar until light in colour. Add the egg and vanilla essence gradually, beating continuously. Sift flour and almonds and mix until suitable for piping, adding pepper. Pipe on to a lightly greased tray using whatever shape nozzle you like and decorate with half the almonds. (Heart-shaped biscuits make a beautiful Valentine's Day dessert.) Bake for about 10 minutes. When cooked, remove on to a wire rack to cool.

To make the Champagne Sabayon: Place half the sugar in a pot with the champagne and bring to the boil. Soften the gelatine in cold water and add to the champagne and sugar. In a mixer, whisk the egg yolk and cheese and gradually incorporate the wine and sugar mix. Allow mix to become totally cool before stopping mixer — 10 minutes. In another bowl, whisk the egg-whites with the remainder of the sugar until they form stiff peaks. Fold the egg-white into the egg yolk mixture, followed by the cream, and leave in the fridge for approximately 30 minutes before use.

Place the biscuits in the centre of the plate and pile on a generous portion of strawberries. Spoon the sabayon around the plate and place under a hot grill for about 60 seconds until golden brown.

Top with freshly whipped cream and plenty of icing sugar and serve with a long chilled glass of bubbly!

Clementine Gratin with Sabayon of Cointreau

Serves 6–8

20 clementines (or satsumas)
200 g sugar and 120 g sugar
1 litre Muscat Baumes de Venise wine
10 egg yolks
4 measures Cointreau
2 star anise
1 cinnamon stick
2 cardamom pods, crushed
1 vanilla pod

In a large saucepan, boil the wine, sugar, star anise, cinnamon stick, cardamom and vanilla pod. Once boiled, peel the clementines with a sharp knife. Remove the white pith, leaving the flesh, and put into the hot wine mixture. Leave for 30 minutes.

In another bowl, whisk the egg yolks and 120 g sugar, set over simmering water, and whisk vigorously for 3 minutes, being careful not to curdle the eggs. Remove from heat and add the Cointreau. Place the bowl on a cloth and with an electric mixer whisk the mix again until cold, light and fluffy.

Place a portion of 3–5 clementines in a bowl, spoon over the sabayon (the sauce should coat the clementines). Place under a hot grill to crisp the top. Sprinkle with icing sugar and serve immediately.

NB: Peaches or apricots can be substituted for clementines. Green or black grapes may also be used, but need to be skinned first.

Caramelised Orange Shortbread Tartlet

Serves 10

Pastry

250 g plain flour
175 g unsalted butter, in pieces
75 g caster sugar
zest of 2 oranges, finely grated
10 ml cold water

Filling

550 ml double cream
1 vanilla pod, split
4 large egg yolks
125 g caster sugar
rind and juice of 1 orange

Heat oven to 200°C/400°F/Gas 6. To make pastry, put the flour in a food processor, add the butter and process until the mixture resembles breadcrumbs. Add the sugar, orange zest and water and process briefly until a firm dough is formed. Wrap and chill for 30 minutes. Roll out shortbread fairly thinly on a lightly floured surface and use to line 10 well-greased tartlet tins. Bake for about 15 minutes until pale golden. Leave to cool and then carefully remove from the tins.

For the Filling: Heat oven to 110°C/250°F/Gas ½. In a pot, heat cream, sugar, vanilla pod and orange to boiling point. Turn off heat and leave to infuse for 15 minutes. Beat eggs gently and then add cream. Strain through a fine sieve and allow to cool. Pour mixture into pre-baked shortbread and bake for 50 minutes to an hour. Remove from oven and allow to cool before placing under a hot grill to caramelise.

Chocolate Fig Brownies with Frozen Raspberry Pâté

Make this a day in advance.
Serves 12

Chocolate Fig Brownies
150 g unsalted butter
200 g Bournville or Belgian chocolate
(70% cocoa solids)
5 eggs, medium to large
175 g caster sugar
200 g self-raising flour
2 teaspoons vanilla essence
100 g nuts, chopped (optional)
200 g dried figs, chopped
icing sugar and cocoa powder

Raspberry Pâté *(makes one terrine)*
450 g raspberries, fresh or frozen
6 leaves gelatine
4 egg yolks
75 g caster sugar
550 ml double cream

Heat oven to 170°C/325°F/Gas 3. Grease a 20.5 cm square tin and line the bottom with greaseproof paper. Melt butter and chocolate in a bowl over a pot of boiling water and stir until smooth. Whisk sugar and eggs on high speed for about 10 minutes until thick, pale and frothy. Mix in the vanilla essence and melted chocolate mixture. Sift and lightly fold in the flour, adding the nuts and figs. Pour mixture into the prepared tin and bake in the preheated oven for 45–50 minutes until set. Leave to cool in the tin, then transfer on to a wire rack. Cut into squares and dust with icing sugar and cocoa powder.

To make Raspberry Pâté: Bring raspberries to the boil in a pot with a little water. Turn off heat and allow to cool. Semi-whip cream and leave in fridge. Place gelatine in a pot of cold water until it softens, then remove water and melt gelatine over a basin of boiling water. Whisk the egg yolks and sugar on high speed until thick and frothy — about 12 minutes. Add the gelatine to the warm raspberry mixture, then fold this into the egg mixture until fully incorporated. Finally, fold in the whipped cream. Line a 900 g bread tin with cling film, pour in pâté mixture, add a few whole raspberries and cover. Place in the freezer for 24 hours. When set, remove from tin, take off cling film and slice as needed.

Autumn

Starters

Stuffed Mussels with Fresh Garden Herbs and Garlic Butter

Creamy Pumpkin Soup with Caraway Seeds

Caesar Salad with Herb Croûtons

Prawn Bisque

Main Courses

Kerry Lamb Pie with Roasted Parsnips

Fresh Grilled Halibut with Orange Butter Sauce

Roast Loin of Venison with Cherry Relish and Celeriac Purée

Honey-Glazed Ham

Pan-Fried Skate or Ray Wing with Sesame Fried Vegetables and Soy Dressing

Pan-Fried Scallops with Grilled Black Pudding and Wholegrain Mustard Cream

Desserts

Chocolate Roulade with Autumn Berries and White Chocolate Cream

Spiced Apple Samosas with Chilled Apple Soup and Lime Crème Fraîche with Cardamom

Deep Rhubarb and Oatflake Crumble Pie with Raspberry Sauce

Sticky Toffee and Walnut Pudding, Rum and Raisin Sauce and Caramelised Apples

My favourite time of the year is September and October and the end of the summer season. You get time to go home, kick leaves, have long walks and meet friends. It's the season for guinea fowl, quail, wood pigeon and sea bass. Plaice, in particular, has a good iodine taste at this time of year. Halibut, which in my estimation is the prince of the sea, comes into season now. I love halibut — it's a meaty fish with a delicate flavour halfway between sea bass and monkfish. You can pan fry it on the bone or serve it with an orange butter sauce. As for turbot, it needs the simplest cooking, because it speaks for itself.

Autumn is traditionally the season of mellow fruitfulness, of making jams, chutneys and harvesting produce from the hedgerows. I remember my father making elderflower wine and sloe gin from jealously guarded family recipes. We serve delicious tangy desserts like spiced apple samosas and rhubarb crumble pies that mark the season.

At Hallowe'en we cut pumpkins and place them as lanterns on the tables and we make pumpkin soup. We serve barm brack with coffee as petits fours, the seasonal touches that our customers notice. Autumn is a good time for mussels and we stuff and grill them with fresh garden herbs and butter. Ham, that most traditional of Irish fare, comes into its own at this time of year, glazed with honey in a cider and mustard sauce though we are more inclined to offer that as a lunchtime rather than a dinner time dish.

When we opened in November 1992, one of the first items on the menu was prawn bisque and it has, along with lamb pie, remained there ever since, becoming a signature dish of the restaurant. We make it on a fish stock base with the crushed shells of the prawns, a *mirepoix* of vegetables, tomato purée and a good dollop of brandy — a perfect autumnal meal in itself.

Stuffed Mussels with Fresh Garden Herbs and Garlic Butter

Serves 4

Mussel Cooking Liquor

½ an onion, chopped
1 carrot, chopped
2 celery sticks, chopped
1 small leek, chopped
15 g unsalted butter
1 clove garlic, crushed
1 bay leaf
1 sprig fresh thyme
½ bottle dry white wine
600 ml fish stock (see page 126)
1 kg mussels, scrubbed and bearded

Garlic Butter

6 shallots, finely chopped
1 large clove garlic, crushed
250 g unsalted butter
300 g white breadcrumbs
2 tablespoons parsley, chopped
2 tablespoons chives, chopped
2 tablespoons chervil, chopped

Garnish

2 teaspoons fresh parsley, chopped
4 lemon wedges
4 sprigs flat leaf parsley

To make the Garlic Butter: Sweat the chopped shallots and garlic in a tablespoon of the butter until tender. Add garden herbs and breadcrumbs and leave to cook. Mix in the remaining butter.

Sweat the chopped onion, carrot, celery and leek in butter with the garlic, bay leaf and thyme for a few minutes. Add white wine and boil to reduce until dry. Add fish stock, bring to the boil and then add mussels, cover and steam until shells begin to open. Remove from heat. Remove mussels from their shells and keep them moist in a little of the cooking liquor. Rinse the shells, place them on a circular wide bottomed plate or bowl and put mussels in each shell. Top with the garden herb crumbs, then place them under a grill until golden brown.

To serve, sprinkle with chopped parsley and garnish with flat parsley and lemon wedges.

Stuffed Mussels with Fresh Garden Herbs and Garlic Butter

Creamy Pumpkin Soup with Caraway Seeds

Serves 4

400 g pumpkin, cut into 1 cm cubes
1 onion, finely chopped
100 g potato, cut into 1 cm cubes
2 sticks celery, finely chopped
1 clove garlic, crushed
100 ml cream
1 teaspoon caraway seeds
1 litre chicken stock (see page 126)

Heat some vegetable oil in a saucepan, add onion, celery and garlic and fry gently for about 10 minutes. Add the pumpkin and potato and cook for a further 5 minutes before pouring in chicken stock and caraway seeds. Bring to the boil and simmer for 45 minutes until all the vegetables have softened. Liquidise, return to saucepan, add cream and reheat.

Ladle into bowls and serve.

Caesar Salad with Herb Croûtons

Serves 4

2 cos lettuces, washed and cut into 4 cm pieces
50 g Parmesan cheese shavings
4 slices herb bread (see page 27)
Caesar dressing (see recipe)

Caesar Dressing
2 egg yolks
4 anchovies
1 clove garlic, crushed
50 ml white wine vinegar
50 g Parmesan cheese, grated
200 ml sunflower oil
4 drops Worcester sauce

To make the Caesar Dressing: Place all ingredients except sunflower oil in a liquidiser and blend. With the motor still running, slowly add the oil, then season with salt and pepper to taste.

To make the Herb Croûtons: Heat oven to 170°C/325°F/Gas 3. Cut the bread into 1 cm squares, place on a baking tray and bake for about 20 minutes, turning occasionally. Leave to cool. Mix the lettuce and half the Parmesan shavings together in a bowl, add the dressing and toss well.

To serve, transfer the salads into deep soup plates or pasta bowls and sprinkle with the herb croûtons and remaining Parmesan cheese.

Prawn Bisque

Serves 4

25 g butter
2 onions
2 white of leek
bouquet garni
20 prawn shells
4 carrots
1 clove garlic
1 litre fish stock (see page 126)
8 celery stalks
1 tablespoon tomato purée
2 tomatoes
1 tablespoon flour
1 teaspoon salt and pepper
1 star anise
1 tablespoon fennel seeds
1 fennel bulb
2 tablespoons brandy

Chop the onion, celery, leek, carrot, garlic and fennel, and cook in a pot with butter and bouquet garni under a low heat until the vegetables are soft. Add tomato, prawn shells, purée and flour and cook for a further 5 minutes. Add fish stock, bring to the boil and allow to simmer for 10 minutes. Remove from heat, strain through a sieve or conical strainer. Season to taste and add brandy.

To serve, add a dash of pouring cream and chopped parsley.

Prawn Bisque

Kerry Lamb Pie with Roasted Parsnips

Serves 4

750 g diced leg of lamb
bouquet garni
10 button mushrooms
2 carrots
2 onions
4 sticks celery
700 ml chicken stock (see page 126)
200 ml white wine
1 teaspoon gravy browning
1 dessertspoon tomato purée
15 g butter
1 large or two small parsnips, diced and roasted in butter
4 saucer-sized discs puff pastry, to cover four soup bowls
1 egg, beaten

Heat oven to 200°C/400°F/Gas 6. Chop vegetables into chunky pieces. Cut mushrooms in half and sauté in a little oil for about 10 minutes. Seal the lamb in a hot saucepan with a small amount of oil, season with salt and pepper and cook for 4–5 minutes. Add onion, carrot and celery and cook with the lamb for a further 5 minutes. Add tomato purée, cook for a further 2–3 minutes, then pour in chicken stock, gravy browning and white wine. Bring to the boil and simmer for about one hour until tender. Add bouquet garni and cooked button mushrooms. Roll out pastry slightly bigger than serving bowl. Pan-fry parsnips in some butter until tender. Ladle lamb pie into the bowl, top with parsnips and cover with the pastry. Brush with beaten egg and bake for 20 minutes until pastry is golden brown.

Kerry Lamb Pie with Roasted Parsnips

Fresh Grilled Halibut with Orange Butter Sauce

Serves 4

4 x 180 g portions halibut
100 g unsalted butter
2 small shallots, finely chopped
5–6 green peppercorns
1 bay leaf
1 star anise
2 strips orange zest
3 tablespoons brandy
glass white wine
200 ml orange juice
100 ml chicken stock (see page 126)
100 ml white wine vinegar
salt and pepper

Butter halibut and season with salt and pepper. Place under grill and cook on both sides for 3–4 minutes until golden brown.

To make Orange Butter Sauce: Heat a little butter in a pot with shallots, peppercorns, bay leaf, star anise and orange zest, and cook until tender. Add brandy and wine and reduce until almost dry, then add vinegar and orange juice. Chop up remaining butter and whisk it into the sauce, then strain through a sieve. Add salt and pepper to taste.

Roast Loin of Venison with Cherry Relish and Celeriac Purée

Serves 4

4 x 150 g venison, boned and trimmed
60 g unsalted butter
300 ml red wine and six juniper berries*
1 sprig rosemary and thyme*
2 bay leaves*
180 g cherry relish (see recipe)
120 g celeriac purée (see recipe)
*marinade

Cherry Relish (can be made in advance)
100 g unrefined demerara sugar
175 ml cider vinegar
75 g onions, finely chopped
1 orange rind, finely grated
2 teaspoons ground cinnamon
2 teaspoons ground allspice
450 g morello cherries
sea salt and black pepper

Celeriac Purée
1 big head celeriac (or two small)
150 ml cream
1 clove garlic
salt, pepper and thyme
1 bay leaf
50 g butter

Heat oven to 200°C/400°F/Gas 6. Marinate the loins of venison in the red wine, thyme, rosemary, bay leaf and juniper berries for 24 hours. Remove venison from the marinade and pat dry on kitchen paper. Retain marinade. Seal the venison on all sides in a very hot pan with a little oil and place in the oven, turning occasionally until cooked to your liking. When venison is cooked, remove and set aside on a warm plate. Drain the cooking pan of all grease and add marinade. Reduce to sauce consistency and pass through a fine sieve.

To make the Cherry Relish: Put all the ingredients in a heavy based pan and simmer for 40 minutes.

To make the Celeriac Purée: Dice celeriac and garlic and sweat in butter with bay leaf until tender. Remove bay leaf, mash and blend in cream.

To serve, arrange celeriac purée in the centre of the plate and place venison on top. Whisk unsalted butter into the sauce and spoon over the venison. Add the cherry relish on top or on the side of the plate and garnish with a sprig of mint.

Roast Loin of Venison with Cherry Relish and Celeriac Purée

Honey-Glazed Ham

Serves 4

1 x 900 g cooked ham
20 cloves
400 ml cider
1 tablespoon English mustard
30 ml honey

Heat oven to 180°C/350°F/Gas 4. Remove the skin from the ham, making sure to leave as much of the fat as possible. Run the sharp side of a knife across the fat 10 times lengthways and 10 times across. Place ham in a deep tray and stud the fat with the cloves. In a small saucepan heat the cider, honey and mustard together and pour over the ham. Bake the ham for about one hour, basting it every 10 minutes with the cider mixture.

Pan-Fried Skate or Ray Wing with Sesame Fried Vegetables and Soy Dressing

Serves 4

4 ray wings, skin removed
4 portions sesame fried vegetables
(see recipe)
soy dressing (see recipe)

Sesame Fried Vegetables
1 onion, finely diced
1 clove garlic, crushed
1 carrot, shredded
1 courgette, shredded
50 ml sesame oil
1 teaspoon sesame seeds

Soy Dressing
2 tablespoons soy sauce (Kikoman)
⅓ teaspoon Dijon mustard
2 tablespoons olive oil
2 tablespoons sesame oil
1 tablespoon balsamic vinegar

Heat oven to 200°C/400°F/Gas 6. Heat a frying pan until very hot and add a little oil. Season skate with salt and pepper and seal on both sides. Transfer the fish to a roasting tray with a little butter and roast each side for about 5 minutes until the flesh just leaves the bone when you touch it.

Sesame Fried Vegetables: Heat the sesame oil in a wok or large frying pan. When the pan is very hot, fry onions quickly, stirring all the time, then add garlic and cook for 2 minutes, then the carrots and cook for 2 minutes and finally the courgettes and cook for 2 minutes. Season with salt and pepper and mix in sesame seeds.

To make Soy Dressing: Whisk the mustard, vinegar and soy sauce together, then slowly add the olive oil, whisking continuously. Repeat with sesame oil.

To serve, warm vegetables, place skate in the centre of the plate and drizzle the soy dressing around.

Pan-Fried Scallops with Grilled Black Pudding and Wholegrain Mustard Cream

Serves 4

20 large scallops, cleaned and trimmed
12 slices black pudding, approx. 2 cm
thick
4 knobs butter
salt and pepper

Wholegrain Mustard Cream
50 g butter
3 shallots
½ glass dry white wine
300 ml double cream
1 bay leaf
2 teaspoons grain mustard
300 ml fish stock (see page 126)

Heat a trickle of olive oil in a big pan and when very hot, add scallops and sear for about 2 minutes on both sides. In a separate pan, fry black pudding for 2 minutes on both sides. Place both on kitchen towels.

To make Mustard Cream: Sweat shallots and bay leaf in a little butter for a few minutes, then add white wine and boil to reduce until almost dry. Add fish stock, reduce by half, then pour in cream and cook slowly until sauce consistency. Strain through a sieve and stir in mustard. Some chopped chives and parsley can be added.

To serve, divide scallops into 4 portions and surround each portion with 3 pieces of black pudding and a swirl of mustard cream.

Chocolate Roulade with Autumn Berries and White Chocolate Cream

A finger-licking lunch time favourite
Serves 6

Roulade
175 g good quality dark chocolate
(70% cocoa solids)
150 ml water
6 eggs, separated
175 g caster sugar
1 teaspoon rum essence
dash lemon juice

White Chocolate Cream
300 ml double cream
2 teaspoons icing sugar
75 g white chocolate
3 egg yolks
2 tablespoons Cointreau

To make the Roulade: Heat oven to 180°C/350°F/Gas 4. Grease and line a Swiss roll tin with non-stick parchment. Melt the chocolate with the water in a small bowl over a pan of simmering water. Whisk the egg yolks with the sugar using an electric mixer, beat in the rum essence and then the chocolate. In a clean bowl, whisk the egg-whites and lemon juice until stiff peaks form, then stir in a quarter of the egg-white into the chocolate mix to loosen it up. Fold in the rest and pour mixture into prepared tin, spreading evenly. Bake for 20–25 minutes. When cooked, remove and cover with a damp (not wet) cloth and leave to cool in the fridge for a couple of hours.

To make White Chocolate Cream: Whisk cream and icing sugar together and set aside. In a bowl, whisk the egg yolks vigorously over a saucepan of boiling water for about 2 minutes. Remove from heat and using an electric mix, continue to whisk until the eggs are light, fluffy and cold. Melt white chocolate. Add the Cointreau to the egg mix and fold in the white chocolate until fully incorporated. Now fold in the cream and allow to set for a few minutes before serving.

Autumn Berries

150 g berries (blackberries, red berries,
blackcurrants and bilberries if available)
1 orange, juice and zest
50 ml water
25 g caster sugar
½ cinnamon stick

Autumn Berries: Set some aside for decoration. Bring orange juice, zest, water, sugar and cinnamon stick to the boil. Turn off the heat and add the berries, stirring until they burst. Allow to cool before using.

Dust a large sheet of greaseproof paper with caster sugar, remove cloth from roulade and turn out on to the paper. Fill evenly with white chocolate cream and follow with berry mix. Roll from one end to the other like a big sausage, using the paper to help tighten it. Replace in fridge for an hour before cutting. Remove paper and portion.

Serve with cream, fresh berries and chocolate shavings.

A low-fat dessert, simple to make, inspired by Indian cuisine
Serves 6

5 Golden Delicious apples, peeled, cored and diced
50 g unsalted butter
100 g sultanas
20 g chopped stem ginger
25 g chopped hazelnuts
25 g caster sugar
12 sheets Wonton pastry (spring roll pastry)
2 teaspoons mixed spice
1 egg, beaten

Apple Soup

400 g Golden Delicious apples, peeled, cored and roughly chopped
200 ml flat cider
rind of ½ a lemon
2 whole cloves
½ cinnamon stick
1 star anise
100 g caster sugar

Lime Crème Fraîche with Cardamom

225 ml cream
40 ml buttermilk
juice and grated zest of one lime
1 teaspoon icing sugar
2 cardamom pods, seeds only

To make Apple Soup: Stew all ingredients until apples are soft. Remove from heat and take out cinnamon stick, cloves and star anise. Blend pulp in a food processor, strain and chill immediately.

To make the Lime Crème Fraîche: Mix all the ingredients and leave in a warm place overnight (beside an oven or in a hot press). Stir every couple of hours. You will have crème fraîche the following morning.

To make the Spiced Apple Samosas: Heat oven to 180°C/350°F/Gas 4. Melt the butter in a pot and add ginger, sugar and spice. Dice the apples to twice the size of the sultanas and add both to the pot, cooking for about 2 minutes. Remove from heat and chill in refrigerator. When cool, stir in the chopped hazelnuts. Take one sheet of pastry at a time and cut in half creating a triangle. Place a tablespoon of mix in one corner of the pastry and brush the rest of the pastry with beaten egg. Fold one corner over to another, creating a smaller triangle, and egg wash this too. Press down and continue with the rest of the pastry. Allow 3 for each serving, so you should make 12 in total. Use plenty of flour to dust the samosas as the apple can make the pastry soggy. Place in the oven for 10 minutes or deep fry 2 or 3 at a time in a preheated fryer until golden brown.

Crème Fraîche with Cardamom

To assemble the dessert: Use a big bistro-style bowl. Ladle a good portion of apple soup to cover base of bowl. Serve 3 wontons on top and drizzle crème fraîche around them. Grate some fresh lime over the edges of the plate.

To serve, dust liberally with icing sugar.

Spiced Apple Samosas with Chilled Apple Soup and Lime Crème Fraîche with Cardamom

Deep Rhubarb and Oatflake Crumble Pie with Raspberry Sauce

Makes one 25.5 cm tart (serves 8)

sweet pastry (see page 74)
720 g fresh rhubarb
50 g unsalted butter
75 g caster sugar
1 teaspoon ground cinnamon
1 teaspoon ground ginger
100 ml raspberry sauce
(see recipe)
10 g Marvel (dried milk powder), optional

Raspberry Sauce *(serves 4)*
200 g fresh or frozen raspberries
100 ml water
30 g caster sugar
½ cinnamon stick
1 clove
1 star anise

Crumble Topping
50 g plain cream flour
25 g oatflakes
75 g brown sugar (demerara)
75 g unsalted butter
50 g digestive or any other biscuits, crushed

To make the Raspberry Sauce: Boil all the ingredients to a pulp in a heavy bottomed pot. Blend in a mixer and strain through a sieve to remove the seeds etc. Place in the fridge and allow to cool. Sweeten to taste.

To make the Filling: Wash and roughly chop the rhubarb into 12 mm pieces. Melt butter in a heavy bottomed saucepan and add half the rhubarb, raspberry sauce, sugar and spices and cook until rhubarb is soft and stringy. Toss in remaining rhubarb, turn off heat and cool in refrigerator.

To make the Crumble Topping: Heat oven to 190°C/375°F/Gas 5. Sift flour into a bowl. Mix in sugar, biscuits, Marvel, oatflakes and spice. Gradually work in the butter to make a crumbly mixture. Line a deep 25.5 cm tart or flan ring with sweet pastry, rolling it as thinly as possible. Add in the rhubarb filling right to the top, spreading evenly. Heap a good layer of crumble topping to cover the rhubarb completely. Bake in the oven for about 30–35 minutes until the top is brown and crunchy.

To serve, add freshly whipped cream flavoured with cinnamon.

Sticky Toffee and Walnut Pudding, Rum and Raisin Sauce and Caramelised Apples

Serves 8

Pudding
150 g butter
200 g brown sugar
150 ml water
300 ml single or double cream
125 g dates, chopped
1 teaspoon bread soda
1 egg, beaten
125 g cream flour
50 g walnuts
25 g stem ginger, chopped

Rum and Raisin Sauce
caramel sauce (see page 119)
50 ml dark rum
120 g raisins

Caramelised Apples
100 g caster sugar
dash of lemon juice
50 g unsalted butter
4 Golden Delicious apples, peeled, cored and quartered

Heat oven to 180°C/350°F/Gas 4. In a saucepan, gently warm 125 g of sugar and the cream and bring to the boil. Allow it to bubble for about 3 minutes, then pour a small amount of the sauce into individual pudding moulds or one 900 g pudding base. Put the dates in a pot with the water and bring to the boil. Add bread soda and stir. In a bowl, beat the remaining sugar and butter until light and fluffy, then beat in the egg. Let it stand for about 2 minutes before adding to the dates. Mix for about 30 seconds, then add flour, nuts and ginger. Pour out into the moulds and bake for 30–35 minutes. When cooked, remove from oven and turn upside down.

To make Rum and Raisin Sauce: Make caramel sauce. Poach raisins for about 2 minutes in boiling water, strain and pat dry. Mix the rum into the caramel sauce and add raisins.

To make Caramelised Apples: Melt sugar and lemon juice in a frying pan to caramel stage, add butter and allow to bubble. Add apples and cook for 2–3 minutes.

To serve, place the pudding on a plate, tumble apples on top and ladle sauce over it. Fresh cream can be added. Dust with icing sugar.

Winter

Starters

Quail and Leek Salad

Leek and Potato Soup with Chive Cream

Crispy Duck Wontons with Cucumber Salad and Hoi Sin Sauce

Hot Smoked Fillet of Salmon with Tarragon Mayonnaise and Baby Potato Salad

Main Courses

Baked Breast of Chicken, Clonakilty Black Pudding Stuffing and Scallion
   Creamed Potato

Venison and Pheasant Pie with Roast Chestnuts and Cranberries

Roast Fillet of Cod with Horseradish Cream, Balsamic Reduction and
   Buttered Scallions

Braised Shank of Lamb with Colcannon

Deep-Fried Fish and Chips in Beer Batter with Tartare Sauce and Mushy Peas

Roast Breast of Pheasant, Confit of Pheasant Leg, Wild Mushroom Crustade
   and Juniper Berry Jus

Desserts

Apricot-Glazed Pear, Toffee and Almond Tart

Baileys and Chocolate Brownie Cheesecake with Caramel Bananas

Steamed Belgian Chocolate Chip Pudding with Lemon Meringue Ice-Cream and Hot
Chocolate Ganache

Ginger Crème Brûlée with Redcurrant Ice-Cream and Orange Shortbread

Winter is the time for comfort food which I love, like robust game pies with chestnuts and cranberries, or braised shanks of lamb. And it's a roasting season, not just of meat and fish, but also vegetables like carrots and parsnips, though we also have wintry offerings such as colcannon, braised leeks and red cabbage accompanying main courses. Winter evenings are all about conviviality — big fires, hearty food and wine and good company. It makes me think of being with friends, good conversation, some Stilton and port at the end of the meal, of being in that warm embrace and not wanting to leave.

Certain foods and celebrations mark the season. Everybody looks forward to seeing the first venison and pheasant which go straight on to the menu and to our annual Old Folks Party which Matt Byrne and John O'Sullivan have been organising for 20 years for the people of the inner city. It is done in conjunction with the Glasnevin Lawn Tennis Club of which we are all members — John was an Irish tennis champion. The staff work for nothing, suppliers give food for free and that happy event kicks off the festive season for us. Our florists, Joy's of Ranelagh, put up the Christmas tree and decorations in the restaurant during the first week of December.

Seasonal desserts put me in mind of chocolate and marmalade steam puddings or poached pears in red wine. At Christmas we make Christmas cake and serve it with coffee and candied orange peel as *petits fours*. We also make mince pies and Christmas puddings which we sell at the entrance along with chutneys, cranberry sauces and coeliac cakes or puddings. We do hampers for regular customers. It's a time of the year when the warm, candlelit atmosphere in Roly's comes into its own, while outside in Herbert Park it is cold and everybody is muffled up against the chill. You often catch people gazing through the windows of the restaurant rather longingly at its enticing, welcoming ambience. Christmas Eve is booked up a year in advance and is more like a house party really. New Year's Eve is a gala dinner; people dress up, we have balloons and live music and the champagne flows. Most of the customers are friends, tables are joined up, there's champagne all over the place and at midnight the staff sing 'Auld Lang Syne'. It's a very special night in Roly's for everybody.

Quail and Leek Salad

Serves 4

12 quail eggs
8 quail breasts
200 g baby leeks, washed, trimmed and cut diagonally into 5 cm lengths
2 tablespoons balsamic vinegar
12 cherry tomatoes, cut in half
3 tablespoons olive oil
1 tablespoon sherry vinegar
20 g Parmesan shavings
2 tablespoons chopped chives
handful of rocket leaves

Submerge the quail eggs in boiling salted water for one minute, drain and refresh in iced water, carefully removing the shells (they will be fiddly to peel). Boil the leeks in plenty of salted water until tender but firm. Drain and pat dry. Pour on the balsamic vinegar while the leeks are still warm, then add the tomatoes. Sauté quail breasts for 2 minutes on each side in a hot pan in a little vegetable oil, keeping the centres pink. Mix the olive oil with the sherry vinegar and season with salt and pepper. Pour half the dressing on to the eggs and warm gently in a saucepan over a very low heat.

To serve, divide the leeks and tomatoes between 4 plates, top with quail and quail eggs, pour over the rest of the dressing and sprinkle with Parmesan. Scatter chives and rocket leaves on top.

Quail and Leek Salad

Leek and Potato Soup with Chive Cream

Serves 4

300 g potatoes, peeled and cut into 2 cm approx. cubes
400 g leeks, washed and chopped
1 onion, finely diced
1 clove garlic, chopped
1 small bunch chives, chopped and mixed together with
200 ml whipped cream
1 litre chicken stock or water (see page 126)

Heat some vegetable oil in a saucepan and gently sauté the chopped onion for 10 minutes, then add garlic and cook for a further 2 minutes. Add the cubed potatoes and chicken stock, bring to the boil and allow to simmer for 15 minutes before tossing in chopped leeks and cooking for a further 15–20 minutes. Remove from heat and blend in a food processor.

To serve, ladle soup into 4 bowls with a spoonful of chive cream on top.

Crispy Duck Wontons with Cucumber Salad and Hoi Sin Sauce

Serves 4

3 duck legs confit (see recipe)
140 g cucumber, shredded
60 g scallions, shredded
6 sheets spring roll pastry
80 g Hoi Sin sauce
egg wash

Duck Confit

¾ litre duck fat or chicken stock (see page 126)
3 legs of duck
50 g sea salt
2 sprigs thyme
1 clove garlic, crushed

To make Duck Confit: Mix together salt, thyme and garlic, rub on to duck legs and leave overnight. Heat oven to 140°C/275°F/Gas 1. Scrape off mixture and put duck legs in a deep Pyrex dish. Cover with duck fat or chicken stock and cook very slowly for 2½–3 hours until the meat is very tender, making sure the cooking liquid doesn't boil or simmer.

Remove bones from duck legs and shred the meat. Mix with 60 g cucumber, 30 g scallions and 40 g Hoi Sin sauce. Separate the 6 sheets of pastry and cut them into quarters. Overlap 2 squares on top of each other, bringing corners in to form a purse shape. Divide the duck mix between them and brush about one spoonful of egg wash on the corners and close. To cook, put them in a deep fat fryer until golden brown and crispy.

To serve, drizzle 4 plates with the remaining Hoi Sin sauce, put the remainder of the cucumber and scallions in the centre of each plate and 3 wontons around them.

Crispy Duck Wontons with Cucumber Salad and Hoi Sin Sauce

Hot Smoked Fillet of Salmon with Tarragon Mayonnaise and Baby Potato Salad

Serves 4

Hot Smoked Salmon
1 wok with lid and steam grill
4 x 100 g fillets salmon
400 g sawdust (oak is best)
50 ml olive oil
salt and pepper

4 x 100 g salmon fillets, smoked
(see recipe)
300 g baby potatoes, peeled and cooked
130 g tarragon mayonnaise (see recipe)
1 small red onion, finely diced
3 spring onions, finely sliced
100 ml Roly's house dressing (see recipe)
60 g mixed salad leaves

Tarragon Mayonnaise *(makes 150–200 ml)*
1 egg yolk
1 tablespoon Dijon mustard
2 tablespoons vinegar
125 ml sunflower oil
1 bunch tarragon, chopped

Roly's House Dressing *(makes 300 ml)*
1 egg
2 teaspoons wholegrain mustard
2 teaspoons Dijon mustard
½ teaspoon English mustard
2 teaspoons honey
2 tablespoons white wine vinegar
300 ml sunflower oil

To smoke the Salmon: Put the sawdust in the bottom of the wok with the steam grill inserted and cover. Heat wok on a medium heat until it starts to smoke. Brush the salmon fillets with olive oil, season with salt and pepper and put them on the steam grill. Reduce heat to low, and with the lid on the wok, smoke the salmon for 6–8 minutes each side, depending on thickness. Remove salmon and set aside. It can be smoked up to one day in advance.

To make Tarragon Mayonnaise: Mix the egg yolk, mustard and vinegar in a bowl using a whisk or electric hand mixer, then add oil drop by drop until the mixture has a thick consistency. Add the chopped tarragon and season with salt and pepper.

To make Roly's House Dressing: Whisk all ingredients except the sunflower oil in a bowl until blended. Gradually add the oil, still whisking, and then season with salt and pepper to taste. Store in the fridge.

Heat smoked salmon fillets in a hot oven 200°C/400°F/Gas 6 for 10 minutes or under the grill brushed with a little olive oil. Mix the cooked potato, red onion, spring onions and about one-third of the tarragon mayonnaise together and season with salt and pepper.

To serve, divide potato salad between 4 plates. Mix the salad leaves with Roly's house dressing and arrange on top of the potato salad. Place the warm smoked salmon on top and drizzle with the remaining mayonnaise.

Baked Breast of Chicken, Clonakilty Black Pudding Stuffing and Scallion Creamed Potato

Serves 4

4 x 200 g breasts of chicken, with skin on
250 g Clonakilty black pudding stuffing
(see recipe)
200 g scallion creamed potato
(see recipe)

Stuffing
100 g Clonakilty black pudding
50 g breadcrumbs
50 g chopped onion
25 g butter
2 tablespoons Lea & Perrins Worcester
sauce
1 egg

Scallion Creamed Potato
750 g potatoes
1 bunch scallions (spring onions),
chopped
50 g butter
100 ml double cream

To make the Stuffing: Melt butter in a saucepan, add onions and fry slowly until soft. Remove skin from black pudding, crumble into the pot with the onions and cook slowly for 5–10 minutes. Remove from heat and add breadcrumbs, egg and Worcester sauce, season with salt and pepper and mix well. Set aside to cool.

Heat oven to 200°C/400°F/Gas 6. Loosen skin on one side of the chicken breast and put 25 g of stuffing between skin and chicken flesh, making sure to flatten it out evenly. Seal the chicken on both sides in a little oil in a frying pan, then place skin side down on a buttered roasting tin. Roast for 25 minutes approximately.

To make the Scallion Creamed Potato: Cook potatoes in salt water, drain and dry out on a low heat. Add the cream and butter and mash. Stir in scallions and season with salt and pepper.

To serve, warm the scallion creamed potato and divide between 4 plates using a pastry cutter to shape, and put chicken on top.

Venison and Pheasant Pie with Roast Chestnuts and Cranberries

Serves 4

4 oven-proof soup bowls
250 g diced venison leg
250 g diced pheasant
1 onion, roughly chopped
1 carrot, roughly chopped
4 sticks celery, chopped
10 button mushrooms, quartered
600 ml chicken stock (see page 126)
200 ml red wine
1 spoonful gravy browning
1 tablespoon tomato purée
1 sheet puff pastry
100 g cranberries
12 chestnuts, roasted
egg wash

In a hot, heavy bottomed saucepan, brown the pheasant in a little vegetable oil, remove and set aside. In the same hot saucepan, brown the diced venison and add mushroom, onion, carrot and celery and cook for 5 minutes, stirring 4 to 5 times. Add tomato purée and cook for a further 2–3 minutes, then add the red wine and chicken stock and bring to the boil. Simmer for about one hour until tender, adding the pheasant after half an hour and the cranberries after 50 minutes. Heat oven to 200°C/400°F/Gas 6. Cut out the pastry slightly bigger than the soup bowls and egg wash around the perimeter of one side. Ladle pie mix into the bowls, top each with 3 roast chestnuts and cover with pastry, egg washed side down. Egg wash the top and bake for 20 minutes.

Roast Fillet of Cod with Horseradish Cream, Balsamic Reduction and Buttered Scallions

Serves 4

4 x 150 g fillets cod
4 portions horseradish cream (see recipe)
16 scallions, blanched and refreshed
4 portions balsamic reduction (see recipe)
20 g butter
juice of ½ lemon

Horseradish Cream
100 ml cream
½ eating apple, chopped
½ teaspoon crushed ginger
1 clove garlic, crushed
½ tablespoon horseradish sauce
juice of ½ lemon
pinch paprika
salt and pepper

Balsamic Reduction
200 ml balsamic vinegar
1 teaspoon brown sugar
1 teaspoon honey
1 teaspoon lemon juice

Melt the butter in a large non-stick pan and add the cod, skin side down, and cook for 4–5 minutes on each side, depending on thickness. Squeeze the lemon juice over them and keep warm. Warm the cooked scallions in a small pan or microwave with a little knob of butter.

To make the Horseradish Cream: Mix all the ingredients except the cream in a blender, whiz in cream for 5 seconds. Pass through a fine sieve and whisk until soft.

To make the Balsamic Reduction: Simmer all the ingredients for about 10 minutes until reduced to a syrup.

To serve, divide the horseradish cream between 4 plates, put 4 scallions in the centre of each plate, place cod on top and drizzle over the balsamic reduction.

Roast Fillet of Cod with Horseradish Cream, Balsamic Reduction and Buttered Scallions

Braised Shank of Lamb with Colcannon

Serves 4

4 medium-sized lamb shanks
1 onion, roughly chopped
2 carrots, roughly chopped
2 sticks celery, chopped
4 cloves garlic, roughly chopped
1 sprig fresh thyme
1 sprig fresh rosemary
1 tablespoon tomato purée
1 glass dry white wine
4 portions colcannon (see recipe)
1 litre chicken stock (see page 126)
salt and pepper

Colcannon
200 g potato, peeled and cubed
100 g curly kale, blanched and refreshed
1 onion, finely diced and cooked in butter
50 g butter
150 ml double cream
salt and pepper

Heat oven to 170°C/325°F/Gas 3. Heat some vegetable oil in a frying pan and seal all sides of the lamb shanks. Remove to a deep Pyrex dish. Add vegetables to the pan and cook for 5 minutes, stirring all the time so that they brown evenly all over. Stir in tomato purée, white wine and reduce by half. Add chicken stock, thyme and rosemary and pour over lamb shanks. Cover and braise in the oven for 2 hours approximately until tender. The cooking liquid should be just simmering. The lamb should be turned 4 or 5 times. Remove, pass cooking liquid through a fine sieve and reduce until gravy consistency and season to taste.

Note: Any fat or scum should be skimmed off while shanks are being turned.

To make Colcannon: Cook the potatoes in salted water, drain and dry out on a low heat. Add cream and butter and mash. Stir in the cooked kale and onion and season to taste.

To serve, divide the colcannon between 4 plates or bowls, put a lamb shank on top and surround with sauce.

Deep-Fried Fish and Chips in Beer Batter with Tartare Sauce and Mushy Peas

Serves 4

4 x 150 g fillets haddock, skinned and deboned
50 g flour
beer batter (see recipe)
4 portions chips
1 lemon, cut into wedges
tartare sauce (see recipe)
mushy peas (see recipe)

Beer Batter
300 ml beer
250 g self-raising flour
¼ teaspoon salt

Tartare Sauce *(makes 300 ml)*
2 egg yolks
4 tablespoons vinegar
250 ml sunflower oil
2 gherkins, chopped
50 g capers
1 tablespoon chopped parsley
½ an onion, finely chopped

Mushy Peas
200 g Marrowfat peas, soaked overnight
1 white onion, finely chopped
¼ litre approx. chicken stock (see page 126)
50 g butter
chopped mint

To make Tartare Sauce: Mix the egg yolks, mustard and vinegar in a bowl, using a whisk or electric hand mixer. Add oil drop by drop until the mixture has a thick consistency. Stir in the rest of the ingredients and season with salt and pepper.

To make Beer Batter: Put the flour in a bowl and whisk in beer and salt.

Heat oven to 200°C/400°F/Gas 6. Dust the fillets of haddock with flour and dip them one by one into the batter, letting excess batter drip off. Using tongs, insert fish into a hot deep fat fryer (about 200°C/400°F), holding them off the bottom until they start to float. Let them fry for about 4–5 minutes until the batter is golden brown and crispy, then place on a baking tray. (You should be able to cook 2 or 3 at a time, depending on the size of your fryer.) When all the fish is cooked, put them on a tray in the hot oven to keep warm. Cook the chips.

To make Mushy Peas: Melt the butter in a saucepan, add the onion and fry without colouring until the onion is soft. Add peas and stock, cover and cook slowly for about 30 minutes until peas are soft. Remove the lid every 5 minutes and stir. Add a little chopped mint to the peas for added flavour.

To serve, divide the chips, peas, tartare sauce and lemon wedges between 4 plates and place the fish on top.

Deep-Fried Fish and Chips in Beer Batter with Tartare Sauce and Mushy Peas

Roast Breast of Pheasant, Confit of Pheasant Leg, Wild Mushroom Crustade and Juniper Berry Jus

Serves 4

4 pheasant crowns (legs separate)
pinch sea salt and ground pepper
whole juniper berries
4 x 50 g butter
vegetable oil

Confit of Pheasant
8 pheasant legs
1 teaspoon crushed juniper berries
1 teaspoon sea salt
1 teaspoon crushed peppercorns
1 sprig rosemary and thyme
½ teaspoon star anise
1 bay leaf
3 cloves garlic, crushed
1½ litres duck fat
150 ml white wine

Wild Mushroom Crustade
200 g shittake mushrooms
200 g oyster mushrooms
200 g button mushrooms
4 shallots, finely diced
2 cloves garlic, crushed
1 bunch spring onions, chopped
1 tablespoon chopped tarragon
250 ml red wine
20 g brown sugar
1 shallot, sliced
1 tablespoon olive oil
4 sheets filo pastry

To make Confit of Pheasant: Melt duck fat at 100°C/210°F. Remove skin from the legs, place the legs in a bowl with salt, wine, bay leaf, peppercorns, rosemary, thyme, garlic and star anise. Rub all the ingredients into the legs and leave for approximately 2 hours, covering the bowl with cling film. Preheat oven to 130°C/250°F/Gas 2. Remove legs from marinade and pat dry with a cloth. Put legs into a casserole with melted duck fat, cover with a tight-fitting lid and cook for approximately 1½–2 hours. When cooked, the pheasant meat should fall off the bone. Set aside to cool. Strain duck fat and store in fridge.

To make Wild Mushroom Crustade: In a heavy bottomed saucepan, put the wine, sugar and sliced shallots and reduce slowly by half. Heat olive oil in a large saucepan and fry diced shallots and garlic well. Increase heat and fry mushrooms until golden brown. Add spring onions and herbs, remove from heat and season to taste.

Preheat oven to 180°C/350°F/Gas 4. Mix together the mushroom mix and the pheasant confit, add warmed red wine, allow to cool, then refrigerate. Cut filo pastry into 15 cm squares. Place the pheasant and mushroom mixture in the centre, brush edges with melted butter and close corners together into a parcel. Bake for 7–10 minutes until pastry is golden brown.

Pheasant and Juniper Berry Jus

4 pheasant carcasses
1 onion, finely sliced
1 carrot, finely sliced
2 sticks celery, sliced
2 cloves garlic, crushed
100 g juniper berries, crushed
200 ml dry gin
50 ml port
20 g tomato purée
1 tablespoon redcurrant jelly
rind of 1 orange
500 ml beef stock (see page 125)

To make Pheasant and Juniper Berry Jus: Fry the pheasant bones (like the wings, for example) in very hot oil until well coloured. Strain off excess fat, return to heat and add all the vegetables until brown in colour. Add tomato purée, jelly and juniper berries and cook for about 2 minutes. Pour in gin and port and reduce a little, then add beef stock and orange rind and boil to reduce until 200 ml of jus remains. Strain through a fine sieve.

Preheat oven to 200°C/400°F/Gas 6. Heat a little oil until very hot in a frying pan. Season each breast with salt and pepper, stud the skin with juniper berries and seal the breasts in hot oil. Remove and roast in oven for 12 minutes. When they are cooked, take each breast off the bone and remove the skin. Place each breast into a pan with hot butter to seal each breast and keep it moist, then remove and slice at an angle.

Serve with mushroom crustade and juniper berry jus.

Apricot-Glazed Pear, Toffee and Almond Tart

Though it looks heavy, this is a very light tart with varying levels of sweetness,
perfect for a pre-Lansdowne Road rugby match and very popular on those days.
Make the toffee and tart base the night before.

Serves 6–8

375 g butter
140 g icing sugar
4 medium-sized eggs
625 g cream flour
1 teaspoon vanilla essence
3–4 pears, peeled, cored and halved
(tinned pears can be used)
100 g apricot jam (for glaze)

Frangipane
125 g unsalted butter
125 g caster sugar
3 whole eggs, medium sized
120 g ground almonds
25 g self-raising flour
½ teaspoon almond essence
20 g chopped almonds

To make the Almond Tart: Cream butter and sugar together in a mixer. Add eggs gradually for 2 minutes, then flour. When a pale yellow dough has formed, stop machine, wrap pastry in cling film and refrigerate for about 30 minutes. (You can add other flavours if desired to this basic recipe like coffee or cinnamon.) Grease and line a deep 20.5 cm flan tin and roll out pastry thinly.

To make Toffee: Submerge a tin of condensed milk in a pot full of water and boil for 3 hours. (It is very important to keep it covered as pressure can build up in the can.) Allow to cool overnight. Open the tin and spread a good layer on to the base of the pastry and refrigerate for 10 minutes.

To make the Frangipane: Preheat oven to 180°C/350°F/Gas 4. Cream butter and sugar together until pale and fluffy. Beat in eggs and essence and stir in all the dry ingredients until you have a heavy paste. Spread frangipane on top of the toffee, filling the tart about three-quarters the way up the pastry. Evenly distribute the pears on top of the tart and bake for 55–60 minutes. Remove the tart from the oven and spread immediately with the hot glaze which is made simply by mixing together 100 g of apricot jam with 30 g of water, bringing to the boil and passing through a strainer.

Serve with cream, plain vanilla ice-cream and l'anglaise sauce (see recipes).

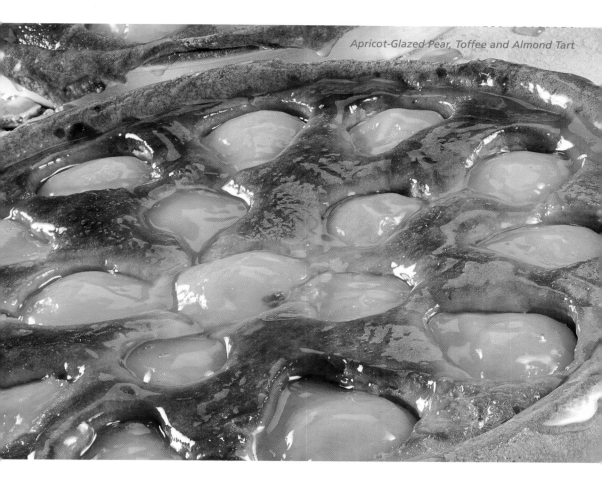

Vanilla Ice-Cream

300 ml cream
300 ml milk
150 g caster sugar
180 g egg yolks
30 g glucose (confectioner's syrup
1 vanilla pod — split in two and the
seeds scraped out

L'Anglaise Sauce

300 ml milk
2 egg yolks
30 g caster sugar
1 teaspoon vanilla essence or
½ vanilla pod

To make Vanilla Ice-Cream: Place the milk, sugar, glucose, vanilla and cream in a pot and bring to the boil. In a separate bowl gently whisk the egg yolks, pour over the scalded milk and mix well together until a thick custard forms.

Place the bowl on top of a pot of boiling water and thicken the custard until it coats the back of a wooden spoon. Place the mixture in the fridge to cool for about 1–1½ hours, then pour it into the ice-cream machine and churn until a smooth ice-cream is formed. Store in the freezer.

To make L'Anglaise Sauce: Whisk the sugar and eggs together. Bring milk to the boil and stir it into the egg mixture. Pour into a saucepan and stir on a low heat until the sauce coats the back of a spoon (do not allow it to boil). Pass mixture through a fine strainer and add the vanilla essence.

Baileys and Chocolate Brownie Cheesecake with Caramel Bananas

Serves 8–10

Cheesecake Base

180 g digestive biscuit crumbs
60 g melted butter
20 g brown sugar
30 g drinking chocolate
15 g chopped almonds
diced pieces of chocolate brownies (see recipe)

Filling

3 leaves gelatine
425 g cream cheese
½ tin condensed milk
550 ml cream
2–3 tablespoons Baileys
vanilla essence (optional)

Chocolate Brownies

150 g butter
65 g cocoa
2 eggs
250 g caster sugar
65 g self-raising flour
1 teaspoon vanilla essence
20 g chocolate chips

To make the Cheesecake Base: In a large bowl mix sugar, crumbs, chopped almonds and drinking chocolate, then add hot melted butter and stir until fully mixed. Spread biscuit mix evenly along the bottom of a 23 cm spring-release cake tin and press it down well while still warm. Keep in fridge while you work on the filling.

To make the Filling: First soak gelatine in cold water. In a mixing bowl, whisk cream cheese and condensed milk together until smooth. In another mixing bowl, lightly whisk cream. Dissolve gelatine with Baileys over a bain-marie and fold gently into the cheese mix. Fold in cream, check flavour, add more Baileys if necessary or some vanilla essence if preferred.

To make the Chocolate Brownies: Preheat oven to 170°C/325°F/Gas 3. Whisk eggs and sugar until pale and light. Melt butter in a heavy bottomed saucepan to boiling point, allow to cool then add to egg and sugar mix. Sieve cocoa and flour together and fold into egg mixture until fully incorporated. Add essence and chocolate chips and cook in a baking tray for 25–30 minutes.

Caramel Sauce

(makes ¾ litre)
455 g caster sugar
60 ml water
1 teaspoon lemon juice
2 tablespoons liquid glucose
360 ml double cream
55 g unsalted butter

Add chopped brownies on to the biscuit base of the ring and pour over cheesecake mix, leaving room at the top for glazing. When fully set, pour over a thin layer of caramel and allow glaze to set fully before serving. Make caramel sauce (see recipe) and slice in 3 whole bananas.

To make the Caramel Glaze: Gently warm 250 ml stock syrup (see page 128) in a heavy saucepan. Soften two leaves of gelatine in cold water and when soft, remove from the water and add to the stock syrup. When the gelatine has dissolved, remove the syrup from the heat and allow to cool. Pour over the cheesecake and leave to set for an hour in the fridge.

To make the Caramel Sauce: Place sugar, water and lemon juice in a small saucepan and bring to the boil. Add in glucose and cook until it reaches a golden caramel colour. Turn off heat and pour in cream (at arm's length as sauce may rise and spatter) and stir. If there are any lumps, return to heat and cook until they are dissolved. Finally, stir in butter. Add more water if you want a thinner sauce.

Steamed Belgian Chocolate Chip Pudding with Hot Chocolate Ganache

Steamed Belgian Chocolate Chip Pudding with Lemon Meringue Ice-Cream and Hot Chocolate Ganache

Probably one of our most popular desserts and a chocolate lover's dream
Serves 8

190 g cream flour
50 g cocoa powder
1 tablespoon baking powder
125 g caster sugar
150 g margarine or unsalted butter
4 eggs
80 ml milk
1 teaspoon orange essence or rind of ½ an orange
50 g chocolate chips

Hot Chocolate Ganache

185 g good quality Belgian chocolate chips (70% cocoa solids)
185 ml cream
30 g unsalted butter
40 g liquid glucose

Beat sugar and butter in a mixer until light and foamy. Gradually add the egg while still beating. Sift the flour, cocoa and baking powder together, slow down machine and add in all the dry ingredients. Add in the chocolate chips and orange and finally the milk. Place mixture in a well-greased l.3 litre pudding basin and cover with greaseproof paper. Tie a string around the basin to secure paper or cover with a weight e.g. a plate. Steam in a bain-marie as for a Christmas pudding for approximately 1½ hours. When pudding is ready, allow to cool slightly and turn out on to a wire rack.

Lemon Meringue Ice-Cream

Make with half the vanilla ice-cream (see page 117), mix with lemon curd to taste (125 g approx.) (see page 49) and broken meringue pieces.

To make Hot Chocolate Ganache: Bring glucose, cream and butter to the boil, pour over the chocolate and whisk until sauce is formed. If it sets it can be microwaved down again.

To serve, portion the pudding, place a scoop of ice-cream on top and ladle over the Chocolate Ganache. Garnish with orange segments.

Ginger Crème Brûlée with Redcurrant Ice-Cream and Orange Shortbread

Serves 8

550 ml double cream
50 g caster sugar
5 egg yolks
2 whole eggs
1 vanilla pod, split and seeds scraped
20 g Chinese stem ginger
75 g caster sugar, for caramelising
8 brûlée dishes

Redcurrant Ice-Cream
550 ml milk
150 g cream
30 g confectioner's glucose
150 g caster sugar
120 g egg yolks
vanilla pod, split and seeds scraped
1 teaspoon vanilla essence
550 ml fresh or frozen redcurrants
extra 130 g sugar

Heat oven to 130°C/250°F/Gas ½. In a deep bowl, mix (but do not whisk) eggs and yolks. In a heavy bottomed pot, heat cream, sugar, vanilla pod and seeds to about 70°C until sugar is dissolved — do not boil. Pour cream on to egg mixture gradually, stirring all the time. Strain the mix into a jug through a fine strainer. Chop the ginger and put it into the base of the dishes. Place dishes on a deep roasting tray and fill with warm water to reach halfway up their sides. Divide custard mix into the dishes, cover the top of the tray with cling film and bake for 45–50 minutes (or if you want them quicker at 175°C/325°F/Gas 3 for 25–30 minutes). Allow to cool until set hard. Sprinkle the top with caster sugar and caramelise using a blow-torch or place them under a hot grill. Set aside for up to half an hour before serving.

To make Redcurrant Ice-Cream: Heat redcurrants (retaining some for decoration) with extra sugar to make a pulp and allow to cool. Whisk together egg yolks, sugar and essence. Bring milk and cream to the boil with the glucose, vanilla pod and seeds. Whisk boiling mixture into the yolks and sugar and blend thoroughly together. Transfer to a clean bowl and gently heat over a saucepan of boiling water — do not boil. Stir mixture continuously until it coats the back of a wooden spoon. Pass it through a fine sieve, leave to cool, add pulp and then refrigerate. Pour mixture into an ice-cream machine and churn immediately.

Orange Shortbread *(makes 20)*

225 g butter
125 g caster sugar
350 g plain cream flour
pinch of salt
rind of 1 orange, finely grated
caster sugar, for sprinkling

To make Orange Shortbread: Heat oven to 190°C/375°F/Gas 5. Cream butter and sugar together until pale and light. Sift the flour and salt together, add to the mixture and stir until it resembles breadcrumbs. Add orange zest and gather dough into a ball with your hands with some gentle kneading. Wrap ball in cling film and allow to rest for about 20 minutes. Roll out on a lightly floured surface and cut required shapes. Prick pastry with a fork to ensure even cooking. Put biscuits on a lightly greased tray and sprinkle with caster sugar. Bake for 15–20 minutes. Remove from oven, allow to cool and transfer to biscuit tin.

To serve, place biscuit on top of brûlée dish and add a scoop of ice-cream on top. Garnish with mint, orange shortbread biscuits and quartered red grapes. Dust with icing sugar.

Stocks

Beef Stock

Makes 3 litres approx.

2.5 kg beef bones (marrows are best)
100 ml vegetable oil
2 onions, peeled and chopped
4 carrots, peeled and chopped
4 celery stalks, chopped
8 cloves garlic, peeled
3 tablespoons tomato purée
½ bottle red wine
8 litres hot water
1 sprig thyme
1 sprig rosemary
10 black peppercorns

Heat oven to 200°C/400°F/Gas 6 and roast the bones until golden brown — 30–45 minutes.

In a large saucepan sweat all the vegetables and garlic in oil for 10 minutes, then turn up the heat and stir constantly until golden brown. Add tomato purée and cook for 2 minutes, then add the red wine, bones, herbs, water and peppercorns. Bring to the boil and simmer for 8–10 hours, skimming occasionally. Pass through a sieve into a clean pot and boil to reduce by half.

Store in a fridge for 1 week, or freeze for up to 3 months.

Chicken Stock

Makes 1 litre approx.

1 kg chicken carcasses, chopped
100 g celery, chopped
100 g onions, chopped
100 g leeks, chopped
2 cloves garlic, chopped
1 sprig fresh thyme
1 bay leaf
2 litres water

In a large pot, put chicken carcasses, add water and bring to the boil. Skim off all the foam, add the remaining ingredients, return to the boil, then simmer for 1½–2 hours, skimming off any fat that rises to the top. Pass stock through a colander, then through a fine strainer.

Fish Stock

Makes 2 litres

1 kg white fish bones (sole is best)
2 celery stalks, finely chopped
1 onion, peeled and finely chopped
4 cloves of garlic, peeled
1 star anise
1 tablespoon vegetable oil
150 ml white wine
2 litres water

Fry the chopped vegetables and garlic in the oil without colouring for 5–10 minutes until soft. Add the washed fish bones and cook slowly for 5 minutes. Add wine, reduce slightly and then add water and star anise and bring to the boil, skimming well. Simmer gently for 20 minutes. Pass through a sieve and leave to cool. The fish stock can be kept in the fridge for 1–2 days or in the freezer for 1 month.

Lamb Stock

Makes 1 litre approx.

2.5 kg raw lamb bones, chopped
1 onion, chopped
1 carrot, chopped
1 celery stalk, chopped
1 tablespoon tomato purée
1 whole head garlic, peeled
2 litres chicken stock (see page 126)
500 ml water
2 sprigs thyme

Roast the lamb bones in a hot oven at 200°C/400°F/Gas 6 until golden brown. In a large pot, sauté the vegetables in a little oil for about 15 minutes. Add tomato purée and cook for 2 minutes, then add the lamb bones and chicken stock. Bring to the boil, add cold water, skim off any fat and add herbs. Leave to simmer for one hour, skimming regularly. It will reduce down to about 1½–2 litres. Pass through a fine sieve.

To make lamb stock sauce, allow 100 ml per person, reduce by half and whisk in a knob of unsalted butter.

Vegetable Stock

Makes 1 litre

1.5 litres cold water
2 onions, peeled
1 bulb fennel
2 leeks
2 celery stalks
juice of 1 orange
10 white peppercorns
20 g parsley, chopped
20 g coriander, chopped
1 tablespoon olive oil

Roughly chop the vegetables and sweat for 10–15 minutes in the olive oil but do not colour. Add water and peppercorns and bring to the boil. Skim. Simmer for 20 minutes.

Remove from the heat and add the orange juice and herbs, stir well and leave to infuse for 10 minutes. Pass through a fine sieve.

Store in a fridge for 2–3 days, or freeze.

Stock Syrup

Makes 1 litre approx.

400 ml water
400 g sugar

Boil water and sugar until it forms a syrup; you could use star anise, cloves and some orange and lemon zest if liked.

Pesto

60 g Parmesan cheese, freshly grated
60 g basil leaves
30 g parsley
30 g pine kernels
15 g walnuts
2 cloves garlic, peeled and chopped
250 ml olive oil

Put the cheese, herbs, nuts and garlic in a food processor. Add half the oil and process until the ingredients are finely chopped. With the processor running, gradually add the remaining oil. Season to taste.

Tip: Put pesto in a plastic squeeze bottle and use it for decorating a plate.

Index